TRANSCENDENTAL Anarchy

TRANSCENDENTAL Anarchy

Confessions of a Metaphysical Tourist

LESLEY CHOYCE

QUARRY PRESS

The publisher gratefully acknowledges the assistance of the Canada Council, the Ontario Arts Council, the Department of Communications, and the Ontario Publishing Centre.

Canadian Cataloguing in Publication Data

Choyce, Lesley, 1951-
    Transcendental anarchy

ISBN 1-55082-073-7

    1. Choyce, Lesley, 1951- —Biography. 2. Authors, Canadian (English)—20th century—Biography. I. Title.

PS8555.H668Z53 1993 C818'.5409 C93-090068-5 PR9199.3.C46Z475 1993

Cover photograph by Roger Davies.
Design by Keith Abraham.
Typeset by Susan Hannah.
Printed and bound in Canada by Best-Gagné Book Manufacturers, Toronto.

Published by **Quarry Press, Inc.**,
P.O. Box 1061, Kingston, Ontario K7L 4Y5.

CONTENTS

TRANSCENDENTAL Anarchy

1
Anatomy of Ecstasy

I've just realized that there is some point in almost any given day when I am overcome by a feeling of absolute, inviolable well-being. It happens sometimes for no particular reason at all. I can be driving down the road. I can be writing a short story or building a wall or simply . . . doing nothing but thinking and, zap, it happens.

Maybe it works this way for everybody. I don't know. Maybe I'm only different in that I see this moment of inexplicable euphoria as part of my job. I'm trying to carve out a career as a writer in the sub-genre of euphoria. So, when I'm emerging from the Penhorn Mall on an oblique and otherwise inconsequential Thursday, I find myself looking off toward the Micmac Rotary for no good reason and suddenly, without warning, certain chemical shifts take place in my brain. I click into sudden cerebral paranormal overdrive. Not only do I ride it out, this minor, quizzical moment or three of ecstasy, but I'm beginning to realize that it is the very meat and potatoes of my financial life.

What I am trying to say is that I actually make my living out of being happy. Go on, explain that to Aunt Alice. But it's true.

9

During these brief, vivid flashes of insight I figure out things that I eventually write about and sooner or later somebody pays me money for what I've written.

There is little need of drug or alcohol to induce such euphoria. The triggers are all around. Music will do it sometimes. Old Beach Boys, even older Bach, Old Time fiddle, or *Auld Lang Syne*, Country and Western bootheel music, or just the usual everyday rock radio jive. Or simply the music of metal on soil as I'm hoeing my garden.

Or — try to figure this one out — I was building the other day with lumber and hammer and nails, adding a new bedroom onto the house. As usual, I wasn't paying close attention to what I was doing. I was distracted by the raven's caw and the cumulus sky when I should have zeroing in on the head of a six penny nail. I had already hit my right hand index finger three times the day before with the hammer, and then once again this morning just to keep in practice. So then comes number five — cold steel hammer head right on target. I yelp. I let out a wild shout of pain and in its wake, as the pain begins to drain away, I'm nearly laughing. I roll around on the floorboards among the discarded bent nails and the sawdust. And — curious as helter-skelter on the half-shell — I feel good. "Am I out of my freaking tree?" I ask myself.

Thank God I dropped out of majoring in psychology in university early enough to do no irreparable damage. Had I copped a B.S. in psych I might try to explicate my moment of euphoria as some sort of sado-masochistic tendency. Or maybe my flights of fancy are a prelude to a true manic depressive roller coaster ride up and down the scale of human emotion.

I think not. Instead, I argue, my persistent, intentional bent on happiness is learned. But then, learning is 9/10ths unlearning. All my life, teachers, experts, and other proprietors of wisdom have been teaching me how to be unhappy. I learned from them how to be a wonderful cynic, for example. I still can be one if I so desire. Sometimes it's fun to be cynical.

I was also in the process of learning to be serious — "to take myself seriously." This is just fine as long as you can have fun being serious. Yeah, fun. Pardon the word. I work hard at what I do but I also cultivate having fun at it.

I had fun the time I rented a jackhammer and tried to pry apart the unwanted bedrock behind my house. Another fantasy brought to life. A virginal jackhammer experience. What a hoot. My stamina was a bit on the short side but somewhere in the heart of the hammer-headed handiwork, I discovered I was having a unique time of my life.

This gets around to a common element in all of my satori experiences. To tap the ecstasy, the cloud has to roll away inside the mind. You have to see a thing or do it as if for the first time. The experience has to be triggered outside but it comes from inside you. And it has to be very close to being fully inexpressible.

Which is why so much of this will sound like hogwash.

I know that some folks get very annoyed over the fact that I get away with what I do. Maybe I'm due for a long prison sentence. I've never been quite capable of "doing the right thing," not 100%. I deviate along the way. And therein lies the fun.

Let me redefine part of the territory of euphoria. Inside the lungs of the moment is a lucid but fleeting belief that *all things are possible,* that a person can accomplish exactly whatever he or she dreams. This is a wonderfully old ragged and tie-dyed myth that I probably got from growing up in the United States where I watched a lot of the early television programming.

There is almost no evidence available that all things are truly possible. Laws get in the way. Laws of gravity, of economy, of colonial politics. Yet the belief persists in me like a crooked toe nail that I've had since birth. It's a mild but persuasive delusion from which springs infinite ways to experience the world. But to this day, I tend not to jump off buildings to test my wings. However, if I do look up at the sky and expect nothing except for it to hang there, suspended for my own use, money will drop out of it.

Money should always be accidental. Occasionally it isn't. Sometimes, you have to perform a task that is designed only to make money. Sometimes it is so horrific, it's like hitting your index finger with the hammer for the fifth or sixth time. And even then, suddenly, it might feel good. But if it turns out to be a long, dull, thudding pain, you have to leave it behind.

If I didn't have this recurring psycho-physical feel of the satori, I don't think I could sustain my hope in the perpetual prevalence of ecstasy. I just know from experience that it's there hovering in the perimeters of my vision and that, if I hadn't kept a look out for it through high school and college and a few rough years of hard work, I probably would have lost it.

In fact, I expect that if you were a voyeur of my day to day humdrum life, you'd see little cause for my endless celebrations. On the surface, nothing at all exciting ever really happens to me. Yet everyday I expect miracles. And the more I expect them, the more they keep happening. If a day goes by and I find not a moment to gape in awe at a pair of herons feeding in the shallows or a chance to suck in the smell of fresh cut cedar, then I'm comforted by the fact that soon something will change. The euphoria will surprise me in some new and unforeseen way. I'll be in the checkout line in Woolco and the cashier from three aisles over will stop in the middle of ringing up three pairs of seamless panty hose and yell over, "Hello, Mr. Choyce. What are you thinking about? I watch your TV show all the time." The crowded aisles of shoppers will look at me and wonder who I am and why, if I am so well known, am I in a line buying a box of Phillips head screws to install new closet doors.

I have a somewhat workable theory that the world exists simply because I exist and I need something to occupy my time. I need other people, entertainment, visual and all sorts of sensorial and sensory stimuli and, if I'm not there to observe and cogitate and get all kinds of excited over these manifestations, maybe none of this interesting stuff would happen.

Of course, the world exists for every other human for the same reasons. We all live in different worlds and our paths just happen to cross.

Living by such myths as I do, one might expect an inevitable downfall. My expectations are way too high, my ego too inflated, my demands too continual, and the endless, if sporadic lightning bolts of euphoria are too cumbersome on the entropy of the planet. Cynicism and despair often find favor over ecstasy. Dull, tedious work wins out over frenetic creation. Like I say, I expect at length to be arrested simply from my lack of human suffering and despair.

If everyone thought like me, what the hell would happen to the economy anyway? I live a sheltered life away from the big cities and big businesses and I expect to continue like this for some time. At night I fall into a deep sleep and dream into extravaganza proportions, all forgotten by sun up. When I wake and confront the evidence of a pristine world around me, I declare myself emperor of nothing and inheritor of good luck. I seem to have some control over my own happiness and the happiness of those around me. Time still eludes me. Still, I feel time's compression and wilt from the brevity all about. And, in fact, if I wasn't expecting several more lifetimes equivalent to this one ahead of me, I could find the whole compact drama just a little bit depressing.

2

When in Doubt Get Metaphysical

L ast week, a man from the Department of Lands and Forests appeared at my back door with two pairs of tethered bird dogs. I watched from an upstairs window as he rang the bell. I couldn't figure the dogs. The man was either very blind requiring an entire committee of hounds for direction or he was up to no good. I associate dogs like these with hunters and I carry around a deep loathing of people who fire maggots of lead into living creatures for pleasure.

At the time, I was trying to write a short story about the afterlife. I was required to leave my character in the long dark tunnel. A voice was very far off at the other end and my narrator had not yet met any spirits or guides. The soul would just have to wait for the author.

At the door, I was greeted by a slightly bald, slightly fortyish Mr. Gilfoy. We had met before but I had since whitewashed the civil servant from my memory banks.

"What we're doing today is a duck count," said Mr. Gilfoy. "We want to find out how many young black ducks there are in the marsh this year and try to figure out why the species is on the decline."

"They are on the decline," I offered, "because men in rusty trucks with high rubber gumboots come out here every fall and blow their brains out."

Mr. Gilfoy thought this was humor. "Well, whatever. We'd like permission to go out on your property and collect a few ducklings, tag them and set them free. Later we hope we can find them again and chart their migration habits and preferred habitats."

"What are the dogs for?" I was a very suspicious man at this point. The dogs were sniffing in the direction of my pigeon cage.

"We use the dogs for catching the baby ducks."

"Not on my property you don't."

I could see that Mr. Gilfoy from the research staff of Lands and Forests had begun to metamorphosize into that sort of Mr. Science researcher who puts on a "Let's be reasonable, Mr. Choyce" sort of smile.

I was simultaneously turning into the rustic homesteader who defends his territory and all creatures who possess squatters' rights therein. I could, in fact, feel my elastic self, my very identity, begin to expand until I was flush with the perimeters of my property. If I could not ultimately defend the entire marsh, I could at least keep the bird dogs off my property and send telepathic messages to the baby ducks to seek asylum therein. It would be the best I could do.

"You mean you use the dogs to catch the ducks?"

"Yes. You see, they are specially trained dogs."

One was pissing on my wife's flowers. "I can see that," I said.

"The dogs retrieve the ducklings and we band the legs. Then let them go."

"Why do you need dogs? These ducks around here you can walk right up to and catch with a net if you have to. I know, I've done it." I was lying. It was a terrible trait of mine when pushed into the pit of an argument with a professional.

"We've tried and it's very hard. The dogs are better at it."

"But don't they injure the birds?"

Gilfoy could see I was headed toward landowner hysteria. He probably thought I had a shotgun inside the door.

"These dogs here have proven to have the softest mouths of any dog in the world."

I laughed. The dogs were slobbering on the flowers now and scratching themselves as Gilfoy bragged about their soft gums and forgiving teeth.

"Yeah, but they must break a wing now and then."

"Actually, we do lose a few that way. Some die from trauma. But we need this information."

"Trauma?" I bleated. Death by trauma . . . what my mother used to call being literally *scared to death*. "I can't abide any ducks dying by trauma on my property," I stated flatly. Funny, I just remembered that my character upstairs languishing in purgatory had died of a trauma of sorts. He had a weak ticker and had been surprised by his wife who often played unhealthy tricks on him, this one involving a voodoo mask and a live chicken. It was intended to be a new sexual experience, but it back-fired.

I began to wonder if I had somehow conjured up Mr. Gilfoy and his four slobbering Chesapeake Retrievers. Had they somehow been punched up by accident from the miscellaneous file in my software?

"Look, Mr. Choyce, I can see that this upsets you, but actually we've found that more die of distress when humans try to catch them. Any ducks that die in our research, however, are put to good use. We take their bodies back to the lab, dissect their crops to see what they're eating, analyze what parasites live in their intestines, that sort of thing."

Gilfoy could tell I wasn't impressed.

"The end result is that we know more about the ducks and their habitat so that we can increase the population."

"The ends justify the means?"

"Something like that. Believe me we use the dogs because they make the job more efficient and do less damage."

There was probably some truth in what he was saying. But my gut reaction was too strong. Underlying his argument, of course, was the fact that if the research was to broaden the population of ducks, to increase their fold and flock, then it was so more hunters could take pleasure in blasting them out of the sky. I could see that here was a man of calm and reason and if I played the game on his turf, he just might win the argument. Dogs would go galloping across the tiny ponds and streamlets that lace my land.

"Yeah," I said at length, "but what does being captured by a dog, even a dog with the softest mouth in the entire galaxy, do to a duck's spirit?"

Gilfoy was caught unaware. I had made a small leap for mankind, for duckkind, and for kindness to animals every-where. He looked me in the eye for the first time, certain now that I was completely deranged.

"Well, I don't know much about that sort of thing." He was stumped. His research had not taken into account the soul of a black duck. I was off and running.

"I mean, I would think that being caught by a dog would damage the spirit of a wild creature. The Hindus believe that human souls sometimes evolve from animals or that sometimes we emigrate back into the bodies of forms other than human."

Gilfoy was shaking his head. "I've never studied much religion. I go to church, though."

"Every living thing has a right to live its life in peace and dignity as much as is possible."

"How far does your property extend?" He wanted done with the argument. He'd get out on the marshland somehow but not across my land.

I stretched my arms wide like an old Indian chief. "I own as far as the eye can see," I said. There was truth to it. A light mist had crept in from the sea and obscured visibility. "Well, I guess we'll have to go somewhere else," he said and turned to go.

"Thank you," I said. I looked out to what I could see of the marsh. If there were any ducks out there, they were hiding. Now it would be much harder for the dogs to run them down and grab them with their rubber teeth. I turned back into the house and let the screen door slam behind me.

As I found my way up the staircase to my fiction, I realized I had learned one of life's big lessons. The way to pull the rug out from under a real professional in any argument was to go metaphysical.

Somehow I had developed a basic mistrust of the rational and the logical. I've only had the briefest of glimpses beyond the surface but I've seen enough to know that sometimes facts are not enough. There are times to make the leap, to get metaphysical, and suppose that we all live larger lives than appearances would suggest.

I could use this in the future. At tax audit time perhaps. Or at any other of life's junctures where men and women hide inside their careers. ("Yes, but what exactly is the spiritual worth of a dollar, these days?") My protagonist, meanwhile, was in the tunnel. I wanted him to see the warm light at the end, hear the voices of fallen loved ones before him and then look back longingly toward his wife in the voodoo mask who would be blaming herself ever afterward. He'd have to return for one more go at life on the physical plain. But upon his return he will have remembered one striking detail, one fragment of knowledge passed onto him from the warm bright bodies on the other side. He will have found out that in a previous life he had been a duck, a humble but elegant common black duck paddling along the shoreline of a pristine lake in Canada on a muted sunny day in July. And his death had been averted by a man who owned the marsh, a man who could not tolerate hard science on his land, a homesteader of metaphysical means who declared he would not allow dogs on his land to catch ducks even if they all had canine Ph.D.s in soft-mouth retrieval.

19

3
Waves of Fear

I was upside down in a kayak the other day and didn't have the foggiest notion as to how to right myself again. I hadn't yet mastered the Eskimo roll but my friend said it was important to get the hang of being upside down in the water. If I got into trouble, he'd paddle over close so I could just grab the nose of his kayak and pull myself back up. Only I tried to surface on the wrong side.

We were in Gaetz Pond in late spring. The water wasn't that cold. Once upside down, the kayak was perfectly content to stay that way. I was fit snugly into its hull and sealed tight with a rubber skirt. I heaved left and right and could get my face within screaming centimetres of the surface but couldn't bend far enough to get a gulp of air. It was a frightening, new situation for me. So I guess I panicked. I thrashed and fought the rubber skirt that sealed me in, squirmed and kicked my legs until I was out, still upside down but out and headed for air.

It had all been a matter of seconds. My buddy chastised me for filling the kayak up with water, and I felt foolish. But it got me thinking about fear.

My daughter had to perform yesterday in a music recital

before a crowd of a hundred or so parents and grandparents. She did just fine, played through the "Cuckoo Song" on the piano and everybody clapped. Sure, she had been nervous but that's what recitals are all about, right?

It reminded me of my own career in public performances. In church and school I had been a master in the art of repeating innocuous poems about spring flowers or playing Joseph in the Christmas play. My Sunday school teachers treated me like I had been born for the stage. I was asked to MC parent's night at Boy Scouts and all sorts of things. It was smooth sailing.

Then one Easter pageant when I was eleven, something went wrong. I was supposed to recite a really dumb poem and I hadn't bothered to fully commit it to memory. The impresario said that we weren't allowed to read from cards. It would have to be memorized. So there I was, headed up on stage and as soon as I had found the microphone, my brains turned to mush. I looked out at the expectant faces and waited for the words to simply leap from my mouth. But nothing happened.

Somebody over near the piano prompted me with the first line and I repeated it but nothing followed. I remembered nothing. Exactly why this sort of thing seemed so horrible at the time is unclear. But it's one of my first clear recognizable moments of fear, maybe even terror. I felt a hot flush of blood followed by an icy, chilling sensation. I was certain that death was close at hand. Instead, only stony silence.

The poem was nowhere to be found in my brain. No one was willing to usher me off the stage. I had been the master craftsman of public performance, a virtual child prodigy in their minds for so long that this moment seemed impossible. The entire congregation had come to expect my clear, strong voice, my enunciation, my ease with four and five syllable words. And now this. I had wimped out before their eyes. A legend was turning to dust. Maybe everyone hoped I would somehow find the missing poem out of the blue or that, better yet, it was all part of the act. It was in the script and somehow purposeful.

But it wasn't. Mr. Confidence had turned to leftover oat-meal. And then, while my mind was still held fast in the beartrap of primal fear that had clamped hard onto my soul, I decided to try something new. Since the poem had been com-pletely erased from my memory banks and since I was physically incapable of moving off the stage, I would have to do something radical. I faked it. And in the process, discovered a tactic that would prove to be my continued salvation throughout my life.

It was the Easter performance so I just made something up. I used words like "dewdrop" and "golden dawn," "daffodil" and "glistening" and "shimmer." "Sunrise" and "sunset." I don't think any of it rhymed or made a single bit of sense. But neither had those corny poems that I was supposed to memo-rize. The ice crackled apart in my veins and I began to breathe again. I could hear blood pounding in my ears and I left the stage, still partly shattered, but a survivor. I knew that the audience was no longer my friend. It was my enemy and I'd be reluctant to do battle with it again.

Paranoia over a similar failure sent me into a temporary retirement from public life. The urgency of that moment's fear was etched with flint into my being. Most other things didn't scare me: bullies, biting dogs, car accidents. Physical pain was no big problem. The very thought, however, of giving speeches made me feel deathly ill.

Going to the blackboard to do math equations was equally terrifying. Numbers took on a life of their own. They appeared malevolent and hideous. I didn't mind answering questions in class concerning what type of government Uruguay had or why the South lost the Civil War, but the idea of an up-in-front-of-the-class presentation was terrifying.

In my second year of high school, an astoundingly demented English teacher decided that we would do debates. We were all assigned an issue and told which side we should argue. This, my teacher Mr. Van Heusen said, would help us better understand the nature of arguments and not just opinions. We were each given a folded slip of paper with our issue on it.

Mine turned out to be "Capital Punishment: Pro." I don't think I had a fully developed idea as to whether I wanted murderers to die or not at the hands of the state, so it seemed reasonable enough to make the argument either way. The day of my debate approached like the final hour of mortal doom. That morning I tried to convince my mother I had whooping cough, but she knew me too well. The morning lasted forever. Lunch gave me a square knot in my gut and then came English.

Debbie Morgan and I would argue in favor of death against Lance Morrow and Vickie Dill. My notecards were all in order. I had rehearsed this speech a zillion times in front of my pigeons. By now they knew all about court precedents and mass murderers.

It started rather well. My opponent, Lance, presented hearsay and bloated opinions backed by little fact. My own comrade, Debbie, seemed poorly organized and almost uncertain as to which side she was on. My other opponent, Vickie Dill, spoke haltingly in a shrill, frightened voice and stumbled through a long list of incomprehensible statistics gleaned from the *World Book Encyclopedia*.

And then it was my turn. I felt perfectly sure of myself, now. Something had come over me. I think it was Vickie's high pitched staccato fear that gave me confidence. I felt cool and confident like the time I had played one of the three Wisemen before a multitude of nearly a thousand people.

I looked at my cards that I had shuffled through hundreds of times before my pigeon flock. I framed the three minutes of sound, rational, articulate and well-informed argument in my mind. And then began.

It was a large class, two classes together actually, as part of a team-teaching experiment. Fifty, maybe sixty students. They were all out for blood. Teenagers feed off of terror. But they'd have no lunch of me. I argued statistics about murder deterrent, gave examples from Georgia and Texas where hanging was still considered fair punishment for major theft. The clock clicked on. I noticed a bored, inattentive audience. Someone was nodding asleep in the back. That meant I was doing superbly. I was zeroing in on an A for the debate. Boredom to fellow students meant an almost certain academic success in my school.

Now I was into my series of poignant, pithy quotes from learned men. I had judges, philosophers, and even Richard Nixon. That's when the vandals in alliance with fear struck again. On the bottom of one note card I had the words, "According to Richard Nixon" and I flipped my card for the quotation only to find that it was gone. My Nixon quote, the apex of my entire argument, was missing. It wasn't there. I had practiced the damn thing so many times and now, just at the critical moment, I was losing control. I was right in the middle of the sentence. "According To Richard Milhouse Nixon . . ." and I had nothing to go on. No memory. And it had been my final point. Nowhere to go after that. I felt the blood go hot, then begin to drain down into my toes again. "According to Richard Milhouse Nixon . . ."

What the hell had Nixon said? Was he even in favor of capital punishment or had I made it all up? I could see the entire class waking up. This was the moment they lived for. I was up against the wall. I prayed to Nixon to come help me out now. Put words in my mouth. *Don't let me melt down into a puddle of melted ego and let the bleeding heart liberals turn the country over to axe murderers and mass killers.* For once in my life I wanted to feel red-necked and arch conservative. I waited for Nixon to save me, but he was nowhere to be found in my stack of cards.

The clock stopped. Seconds expanded into large gaping chasms of time. I could feel the guillotine about to drop the blade, waited for the first whiff of acid from the chemicals below me, waited for the warden to pull the big switch. The audience was alert, senses sharpened to hyper-awareness. They could see the noose around my neck. I felt beads of cold sweat begin to blossom on my brow.

And once again I knew there was nothing left to do but forget the script, depart from truth and book-learned knowledge altogether. I would fake it. I would, in this case, lie to get out of the stranglehold. Who could prove otherwise? Who could know for certain that I had not called up Mr. Nixon on the phone for counsel on this important subject, only to receive this private and privileged informed opinion.

"According to Richard Milhouse Nixon," I began again, "ours is a just and humane society guided by a system of fair and reasoned balance. In order to preserve our very civilized nature, we must maintain a system of capital punishment as an absolute and necessarily resort to punish those elements of our society that would bring down the house of our fathers. The state's right to take away a man's life is a necessary tool of our survival in a democratic society."

Or something like that. I'm almost certain that's what I said. Nixon, of course, had never said anything of the sort. The jocks in the back row all cheered. I had delivered Nixon's words with such impassioned conviction that it was like my several seconds of silence had been a showman's hiatus to build up interest in the climax. It had worked. My three minutes were up. I was allowed to step down from the hangman's noose. My final grade: B+.

After that, the fear began to subside. I would rely on improvisation from then on. Whatever the mistake, whatever the terror.

Very few things make me truly afraid. I've allowed myself to wander into many dangers assuming my naivete and goodwill would always get me through. I hitchhiked through Alabama at midnight, climbed vertical rock faces, went hang-gliding off a mountain. I have been charged at by horse-mounted New York City cops until I was pinned against a glass wall with a thousand other anti-war protesters. I felt the adrenalin rush and a sense of worried excitement but fear stayed mostly out of the way.

Once this year, before the upside down kayak, though, I had a bad moment that brought some of it back. I was in Hawaii, on the north shore of Oahu. It was February and the time of the monster waves of the year. I was out surfing in Haleiwa beside a river mouth along a rock seawall that kept the river from sucking the sand away from the beach. The waves were in the ten to fifteen foot range. I paddled out near the river thinking it was an easy route to take the current out to the break. It was.

Then I watched as the waves slammed like giant fists down over the shallow coral reef. I knew I was out of my element. These monsters had rolled south all the way from the Aleutian Islands, traveled unimpeded from distant, raging arctic storms into these warm waters and now they would jump from a three-foot undulating sea mass into a twelve-foot vertical wall of water in the space of a few short yards. The trick was to catch the wave at the exact critical second, make the turn — even as the top of the wave leaped over your head — and then drive for safety out of the bedroom sized cavern . . . onto the shoulder of the wave and into the calm, deep water.

For some reason I was all alone where I sat. I could see other surfers further west but was glad to have some room to myself. I watched the waves, took a few of the smaller ones and safely made it, all the while watching the shallow water beneath me as the waves sucked out and the coral became all too visible. Then I paddled a little further over and took four deep strokes into an innocuous hillock of water moving my way. I caught the wave, stood up, and saw that I was staring down the slope of maybe the largest wave I've ever ridden in my life. The wall was vertical, already the roof was caving in over my head and there was nowhere to go but down. I dove into the wave, hoping to avoid the coral beneath, but instead the wave sucked me to the top, then over the falls into a maelstrom of hammering white water that punched me around until my lungs felt like they were collapsing. I let myself bounce off of something hard on the bottom. I tried to swim up for air but was caught in the snarling mass of water and kept getting pushed down, down.

Then I felt the demon of fear creeping up into my head and wrapping a chain tight around any hope of confidence I had left. I could sense the doors of bright panic opening. It had been a damn long while since the floodgates of fear had been this far open. I tried for the surface again, but I was still locked under the rolling white water, being carried with it until God knew when. My arms were not attached to my body. My eyes were permanently closed. There was no way up.

And then a funny thing happened. Instinct, practice, whatever. Maybe it was the still-living ghost of Richard Milhouse Nixon lifeguarding the beaches of my imagination. But I decided to let my body go limp. Completely. I relaxed. I pretended I was about to meditate. *Think absolute peace and relaxation. There's nothing to worry about at all. Just relax.* I repeated these words over and over until I actually felt myself sinking. And then the wave gave up its grip.

I poked up for air. The worst of all possible scenarios. Another monster wave was about to snap down on my head. One gulp of air and a deep dive. I went down until I could finger the coral, tried to hold on, slipped but stayed down long enough that the wave passed overhead. I surfaced. Saw my board, miraculously only a few yards away, swam, got on and paddled for sea.

When in doubt, improvise and relax. The two big lessons. I'd paddle for shore, consider what I had learned and find other forms of entertainment. But I had a problem. The waves had carried me into the river current and I was directly in front of the long, horizontal sea wall that was receiving the brunt of the oceanic argument between sea ownership and land preservation.

I tried paddling for the beach to the west but found that it took me back into the heart of the reef-cracking waves that I wanted to avoid. If I paddled east, I would be perfectly in the river current and almost certainly sucked straight out to sea. That would be one option. I had just read in a tourist magazine about what to do if sucked out to sea. "The water is warm," it said, "and if you can simply stay afloat, you will almost certainly survive. A seventy-five-year-old fisherman on nearby Kuaui, for example, fell off the boat. He took off his clothes and stayed afloat for nearly seventeen hours until he was washed ashore. No harm came to him except for the extreme embarrassment he found upon arriving on land naked and having to ask for assistance."

But I wasn't convinced that a long sea voyage, surfboard notwithstanding, was the answer. There were other dangers out there, yet unnameable in my imagination. The more I delayed, the closer I was being washed into the ten-foot high massive lava rock seawall. There were lulls, maybe two or three minutes long between waves, and if I could time it just right, I could paddle right up to the rocks, climb up out of the sea and run for shore. I studied that as my way out, all the while paddling like mad just to stay stationary. No good. If my timing was off, I'd find myself smashed like a bowl of eggs as the waves cracked up against the lava. It was way too chancy.

This left me with one discouraging option. To paddle like a madman away from the river current, back into the line-up of waves from where I'd come, then catch another wave, and hope I could ride it west straight into the sandy beach.

It took a solid half hour of maniacal arm wrestling with water to get me there, and as I arrived at the scene of my initial mistake, I was less than anxious to start the whole sequence over again. Several times I had to scramble farther out to sea to nip over the tip of a critical monster wave about to close out. At long last I saw a gentle little eight foot wave loping my way. Relax, I told my weary self, and you're home free. I relaxed, and I stroked. An easy takeoff, a seemingly graceful exit away from the crashing thunder, then a turn back into the white water, which was taking me at breakneck speed back into the sea wall. I squeaked by the rocks just as the wave gave out and paddled into shore. Most people on the beach had not been aware that anything at all had happened.

Three months later when I shook hands with panic again in the upside down kayak, I came to the surface and thought it through once more. I decided it was good to be reminded of fear and terror. There was so little of it in my life that I needed to keep re-establishing my means of coping with it. The sequence would go this way: fear, terror, panic, relax, improvise, relax some more.

Maybe dying would be just like that and all of this would be much needed practice. But maybe it would be a useful sequence in the avoidance of dying as well — at least until the appropriate moment. Learning to relax in terrifying situations is a major life skill. Pumping adrenaline doesn't always help you think at your best. The next time I'm upside down under water and my lungs have used up all the oxygen I'm going to picture myself in a hammock, strung between two trees on a July afternoon. There's a glass of iced tea sitting beside me and a warm breeze kissing my bare toes. There are birds twittering in the tree tops and the sun is poking little sparklers through the leaves. I don't have a damn thing on my mind but lying there and convincing myself that I'm not afraid of anything.

And if that doesn't work, I'll have to think up something else.

4
Dancing Out of Time

We live in an age of immediate realities, of buying and selling, of concern for immediate reward and pleasure. It may be fashionable to talk or write about angst, about being unfulfilled ("careerwise," as I heard recently) or as a whole person, but, in my circles at least, it remains difficult to communicate about how the individual fits into the linear notion of time that we call history.

I periodically go through expansive phases of feeling that almost anything is possible. If I have an idea or a dream, I should pursue it and, given a little luck, I'll succeed. The notion will crop into my head in mid-commute to a teaching job, or in the centerfold of the night, or in the midst of reading a book or building a wall. It comes from the brain but the feeling is physical, all-engulfing and euphoric. I suddenly realize that I am about to write the best damn novel of the twentieth century or that, with just a little help, I'll be able to eradicate the arms race. Or that, with a little fine tuning, I can rearrange world agriculture so that everyone can be fed.

I really have these moments. Other people do, too. It's just that, for lifetimes, we've been training ourselves to jam the euphoria of possibilities. We do it through seductive day and month-long sessions of mind clutter. My training program, however, hasn't fully worked. Blind optimism and a highly refined ability to daydream has helped to keep my hopes alive. I haven't performed any global breakthroughs yet, but I've been witness to many lesser miracles and even consider myself to be the cause of some. So I still expect great things.

My expansive phases are, of necessity, followed by hours of disappointment. Things don't always work out as planned. But my head seems so jam-packed with expectations, images, ideas, passions, and inexplicable memories that I get the feeling that my life hasn't just begun in a hospital bed in New Jersey in 1951. Nor will it end somewhere thirty to fifty years down the line.

Such musings have, on a couple of occasions, sent me to visit a psychic named Ruth for some insight. I'm a bit of a half-believer in the razzmatazz of mediums, but I find that a new template for seeing the world can always be useful. Psychology, for example, worked the same way for me in college. I read Freud, then Maslow, a bit of Jung, and some of the rest. With each new study, I found a new frame to set the world in. Each made good sense up to a point, and even as I ultimately rejected any dogma inherent in each, I'd come away with a little bit more understanding of the nature of personalities.

But since the metaphysical interests me more now than the psychological, I turn away from science for wisdom. Because I experienced these sporadic golden, glowing, inexplicable moments where I felt I was tap dancing through eternity, then I wanted to seek out a source and an explanation. I wanted to believe it wasn't just a minor chemical shift in my brain, an overcharged gland, or a twinge of arsenic in the water I drank. So I went to Ruth for news of my lives, past, present, and future.

It was February 12, 1987. We sat in a quiet suburban room. I knew more or less what to expect. The floor would not open up and stars would not spin about the ceiling. Ruth closed her eyes and tuned into whatever she tunes into. It begins a little like free association and she relays messages from whomever is speaking to her — usually a familiar spirit whose name I'll call Kirik. As always, I am full of doubts but remain open to possible enlightenment. It's only a short hike between gullibility and plain stubbornness, so I zigzag back and forth along the way. For one like me who believes truth to be such a relative and mutable thing, it's not so hard to both accept and question at the very same time.

I begin by looking for advice. *What am I doing right or wrong with my life?*

"Let me put it to Kirik," Ruth says, eyes like rapid fire behind her closed lids. A pause. "Hmm. That's funny," she says. "All I'm getting is that you should drink more water. Drink more clear water. Is that of any use?"

"I don't know, I'll have to think about it," I say, figuring it can't hurt, wondering if infinite spiritual enlightenment might be that simple. Transcendental water drinking. I say I'll give it a try. "Anything else?"

"Trust your childish, playful instincts."

That sounds good. I like that. Now we are getting somewhere.

After the next batch of advice, however, things are starting to sound a bit too generic: "Look within yourself for answers . . . find your path and stay on it . . . have patience with yourself and others . . . duplication of effort makes for a waste of time and energy . . . know where you are . . . sharpen your tools . . . hone your skills." And then again the advice to drink more water.

I take note of all the fortune cookies thrown my way feeling a little miffed. I guess I am expecting to hear that my next book will be made into a major motion picture and after that I will establish a foundation for world hunger and global disarmament that can, in fact, straighten out the planet. I express my feeling to Ruth that these all sound like pearls of wisdom applicable to anybody on the street.

"That's true," she says, "but consider the source."

"Kirik, you mean?"

"Yes, and he's letting me know he's a trifle annoyed."

"Sorry."

"Kirik says that's okay. It's just that he's three hundred years old and he's been around more than you or me so he might know what he's talking about. Give him a chance."

"I'll keep that in mind. But are there going to be any really productive times in my life . . . above and beyond the usual?"

Ruth looks dubious at first. She frowns. Damn. I am already on a downward slide and she doesn't want to admit it. "No, not right now . . . but there is going to be a very creative phase that will last for twenty years. Probably when you're between fifty and seventy."

"A late bloomer . . . that's great."

"A little late is okay. Don't worry. Were you thinking of going into the clergy?"

"No. I don't know which religion I'd fit into."

"That's too bad . . . but it's okay. Don't worry about the lateness. Sometimes you're too early, sometimes too late. It all works out.

"We've already anticipated ourselves, remember that. What's that, Kirik? Hmmm . . . Lesley, I keep getting this image of chocolate. Is it coming through as a very strong symbol for you?"

I don't eat many sweets. "Chocolate I can take or leave."

The shrug again. "Maybe it's nothing. Just keep it in mind." I take a note just in case chocolate is going to somehow fit into my grand scheme. Maybe I'll accidentally discover a way to synthesize chocolate and feed the world. Starvation would be replaced miraculously by chubby little kids with pimples. It would be a start.

I decide that my time with Ruth/Kirik might be better spent looking into past and future lives, so I ask about the past. Why was it, for example, that I felt compelled to move to Nova

Scotia and, upon arriving here, felt as if I had moved back to a previous home? Why the almost instinctual craving to live by the sea and spend countless hours riding waves winter and summer year round? Why the deep-fixed desire to write, to rebel, to change things. I couldn't tie down answers to any of these from this life. Maybe it had something to do with the *me* from before I was me.

"Help me out here, Kirik," she begins. "Yes, I told him about the water . . . I don't know if he wants more advice . . . let's just see where it goes . . . Oh, sorry Lesley, just fine tuning, I think we're ready . . . In one of your past lives it looks like you lived deep in the forest. A logger maybe. You spent a lot of time shaping things out of wood. Not exactly carving but I get that tactile sense of using your hands to shape things. And I see tall trees. I can't see the time period. Nothing but tall dark trees. Might be spruce trees. Might be Nova Scotia . . . Middle Station or Millford Station. Could be Hants County. You spent a lot of time alone."

"No ocean, though? I could have sworn I was here before like a Micmac Indian or something . . ."

Ruth laughs. "Everyone likes to think they were an Indian in a previous life. I don't know why." I feel humbled. I wonder if souls recycle in ethnic units. I soon begin to see that all of my predecessors were European.

The years are still closed. Kirik is checking into the records. Is he to be trusted? Is he an honest spirit or a trickster? Will he just make something up to please me? Will Ruth?

"Oh, here's something, probably only a lifetime or two ago. You seem to be loading sailing ships in New England. I see the schooners, the warehouses. The docks. Hard work. You don't seem to be a sailor, just a dockworker but you keep climbing up on things to look further off . . . up on rocks, up in lighthouses . . . that might be where the striving comes from . . . you don't rock climb do you?"

"No."

"Well, then it probably is from the past. Hmmm. Oh, there's the Micmac you were asking about . . . No, I think you put that in my head. Maybe you were an Indian but I can't verify it . . . but you were a schoolteacher once, probably in the eighteenth century. I can see you at a desk in a very secluded schoolhouse . . . a quill pen in your hand." Ruth reaches out. "I can almost grab onto it, the quill pen . . . there's a lot of power there in that image. Does it ring any bells?"

"I don't know." I tend to be non-committal. It seems logical that I was a schoolteacher. I accept it now almost as a matter of fact.

"And there you are as a soldier. A Frenchman in one of the wars. You wouldn't believe how many people were soldiers in previous lives."

I don't like the idea. I'm a peace activist, a pacifist. "Are you sure?"

"Yeh, afraid so. Guess you'll just have to accept it. Can't change the past. You can grow out of it, though. Remember, this life frames your next and so on. What you do in this life sets you up for the next. It's really not that hard to figure out from this one what your next one would be like."

That makes sense to me. I keep thinking of Einstein, of the laws of conservation of energy and matter, of physical principles of energy transfer. Everything translates into something else. Nothing is lost.

"Here's a funny mix . . . are you sure, Kirik? . . . Well, okay. Kirik suggests you were a healer once, maybe a medical doctor but probably something older, more ancient." She pauses. "You know what's odd? All of your previous lives were men."

"You mean it's usually more mixed?"

"Oh, sure. I expect, though, that you'll come back as a woman sometime before you're through. It only seems fair."

I don't question what she meant by fair.

"And the other image alongside of the healer is that of a . . . sort of a horse trader, a crafty, sly con-artist. But I can't get

36

much detail on any of these. It's just kind of a fast scan of past lives. Does any of this make sense?"

"Some," I answer. I should be encouraged just to be polite to Kirik but I don't want to prompt anything. The con-artist fits. In this life I am a publisher. Certainly a bit of the old snake oil salesman in me there. How else to be a publisher? Certainly not dishonest but a showman handling exotic wares, yes.

I hear kids outside arriving home from school to other houses. Did Ruth have kids? Would they come home slamming doors, yelling for a peanut butter and banana sandwich and Ruth would have to reply, "You'll have to make it yourself. Right now I'm delivering messages from the fourteenth century."

Like other mediums (media?) Ruth sees herself as a channeller. She believes in her skill . . . has met her guides, first as a child in a near-death experience. The guides have given her insight. There have been a contingent of them. Now she focuses mostly on one, the one called Kirik that she found more agreeable and dependable than the others. Apparently, he doesn't take her over in order to communicate. He just whispers along the news and the images from down the centuries.

"Let's go fast forward into the future, if you will," I request.

"Okay . . . let me just get a fix on it." The words remind me of my father the first time he brought a TV into the house and he tried to line up the antenna just right to bring in Milton Berle. "Oh, Okay, that was simple. . ." she seems to be chatting silently with Kirik. I think they were talking about me, calling me pushy.

"There. I can see three or four more lives on earth.

"That's great. That means no nuclear war."

"Well, not necessarily. Just listen . . . the next life you are very involved in global telecommunications. Very high-tech, very involved with ideas, advancing the technology, linking the world together in a network. You seem very aggressive and always surrounded by equipment.

"After that you retire into gentler forms. Your second life is very different. I see you surrounded by bamboo, or something like it. You carve things, sculpt things . . . out of ivory, I think, and you are living on an island somewhere. It looks Oriental. Pleasant but primitive."

"It could be post-holocaust then."

"Could be, but no one is saying.

"After that I see you as a musician . . . classical perhaps or some sort of very serious music. Do you have musical interests?"

Does a tick hound get ticks? "Yes, I always thought I wanted to be a musician, playing in a rock and roll band. I did in high school. Thought I'd get back into music professionally in this life."

"Well, you'll get a chance at it eventually in the one to come."

But it doesn't sound like rock and roll to me. The image she conjures up is again pleasant but primitive. I see my future self sitting in a translucent geodesic dome playing a sitar . . . something like that.

"Anything else? What happens to me after that?"

I can't exactly remember her words but she indicated that I would go "where we all go" when my days on earth were over. I was too caught up in all the news to probe further. But I wondered about the recycling of the soul. Was earth just a proving ground? Would the soul then move on to more civilized planets? Man appeared so slow to evolve that it seemed reasonable that other intelligent life forms have gone so far beyond us in understanding (not just technologically) that we appear as ants in the anthill.

Or do we just eventually lose the flesh and amble about as spirits?

Ruth had been at it for almost two hours. She needed a rest. So did Kirik. "I'm going to let Kirik go now," she said.

"Any final tidbits ?"

"Kirik says you're going to find something valuable. Something precious. Gold maybe."

"I'm not really interested in wealth," I say.

"He knows. He just sees you finding it . . . on a headland and, perhaps, sticking out of a cliff. Maybe it's just a symbol. Maybe it's not real gold. Like the chocolate."

"Anything else?"

"Just advice: seek the brotherhood of man . . . move carefully but follow your ideas, leave the details to others . . . love your family . . . and yes, Kirik, at the risk of sounding repetitive . . . he says to drink lots of good, clear water."

Ruth shrugged her shoulders, not knowing why Kirik was pushing that point. She opened her eyes and blinked. There had been no trance, no special effects or segregation of personalities, spiritual and physical. I looked down at my notes and thanked her. A few minutes later, back on the highway, the world of the present seemed less real to me than all my other theoretical lives. My foot was dancing nervously on the gas pedal and I was still tap dancing my way through a dozen or so lives backwards and forwards . . . but headed where?

Would I be able to look back from my future life as a musician and remember the *me* of now? Or would they all be absorbed and purged of identity? For the moment, I felt expansive again. I could feel the stretch of time backwards and forwards, the continuity — real or imagined — was linked up through me, right now, driving through Dartmouth and starting and stopping at red lights. It made as much sense as anything I had ever learned in school. Where was the evidence? Everywhere and nowhere.

Suddenly, I felt lonely, for all my past selves. No, I felt cheated. I wanted to be able to pin down their identities, their memory — the teacher, the soldier, the dockloader, the woodsmen and the healer — but their communal lives were nowhere to be found except as they, perhaps, swarmed up in my own personality — my strengths and weakness, my abilities and inabilities, my hopes and my fears.

I now had a whole new set of rules to play by. If I observed my own life, clearly I'd be able to sit down and "anticipate" almost exactly what I would be like in my next life. Or if I charted my personality in this one, I could chart the previous person I was — at least his strengths and weaknesses. I knew that if I had the will, such a tracing would be possible. I could, then, in one sense, communicate with my past selves or future selves through my present self, if I wanted to.

I arrived at work, at the university, and parked my car in the lot. I was really caught up in it now and didn't want to just tap dance, but flashdance backwards and forwards into past and future selves. I closed my eyes as I turned off the key and the images began to swarm in my fertile brain. It wouldn't be until I opened to door to my 4:30 English class that I would realize that I had momentarily lost my current identity. I felt like I was just a smudge in an evolutionary psychic procession, that absolutely anything I tried to do in this world would be of such insignificance (especially writing or teaching) that it would not be worth bothering with.

But I had a few minutes before class started. I walked out into the windowless hallway, bewildered. Students, intent on where they were going, swarmed all around. I found the water fountain, leaned over, drank long and deep in big adolescent gulps. The water pressure kept fluctuating up and down and finally let out a long, cold stream that shot straight up my nose. I wiped the water off my face, I began to laugh. I had arrived safely back at my present self and it felt good to be home, no matter how temporary the visit would be.

5

Creative Anarchy

I was recently accused of being an anarchist and began wondering how I could live up to the accusation. A true anarchist, I figured, didn't live by anybody else's rules. I pick and choose the ones I live by, so I didn't think I was ready to be a card-carrying member.

Somewhere back in university I realized that anarchists weren't merely crazy political lunatics who make molotov cocktails in the back seat of their old Chevies. Oh, it's true, some are. But I don't see them as pure anarchists because they are always trying to impose their will on others and damaging property in the interim. Real anarchists let other people live their own lives.

If I'm an anarchist at all, I think it goes back to a deep hatred of a certain social infliction known as conformity. I believe it was away back there in the cesspools of seventh grade that I was made aware that some of us were conformists who merely went along with the crowd and others of us were, what I would lovingly call, non-conformists. A non-conformist didn't give a shit what other people thought about him. And I aspired to being a non-conformist. There, at the starting block of non-

41

conformity, I guess the guiding principle was clothes. If you wore what was stylish you were simply a conformist and, as a result, would grow up to be a watcher of TV game shows or a manufacturer of zippers. If, however, you wore unfashionable body gear, your parents were either too cheap to buy you new duds or you were, by choice, a lofty non-conformist. I think I was somewhere in between the two.

Despite all the best efforts of J. Edgar Hoover, the FBI, and the CIA, non-conformity spread throughout my American adolescence like wildfire. In fact, it spread through the fabric of the continent until the streets were jammed tight with non-conformity. There was a uniform to it, a basic philosophy and, at length, a political will of its own. By then non-conformity had spread beyond fashion and began to infect the minds of the citizenry. The conformists pulled back into the shadows as our numbers increased until they decided there was no point in dressing up at all or going out into the streets. Some sought shelter by joining the military. Others went into sales and product distribution.

The tide of non-conformity grew, laced with long stringy hair and tie-dyed garments washing up in the shores of every city and suburb. "Christ was a non-conformist," someone said. "Yeh, so was Alexander Graham Bell when he got his start." Great discussions were mounted in the universities about non-conformity. History, it turned out, was strewn with non-conformists. St. Francis of Assisi who spoke with the birds. John Donne, Shelley. Benjamin Franklin for sure. Thomas Jefferson, yes, but George Washington, perhaps not. He was a military dude.

Too much of history sounded like it was full of well-meaning non-conformists who started out bucking the system and ended up inventing the telephone or accepting a boring job as executive in some corporation that manufactured brassiere clips. Non-conformity had run its race, and I was dropping out of the legion. But I had left the world of conformists too many years before to think of being re-ordained back into that fold. I pressed on for a new tack in life.

In spirit I felt myself a revolutionary but there were inherent problems. If I was serious about revolution, I'd probably end up dead or in jail. Both sounded a bit wearisome. I felt handicapped by the fact that I had lived a happy childhood, was not in a visible minority, remained steadfastly heterosexual, and I was not scarred with any major psychological disorders from overusing drugs.

Then I came upon the word "anarchism" while leafing through one of those massive dictionaries in a library:

"Anarchism (*ANURKIZUM*) — the theory that the state should be abolished or replaced by free association of groups (no private property). Differs from socialism in considering the state as intrinsically evil. Philosophic and literary anarchy appeared early (Zion of Citium), political later (Anabaptists, Levelers.) Modern Anarchism outlined by William Godwin and P.J. Proudhon. Violent tone introduced by Bakunin, resisted by Kropotkin. Anarchism suppressed in Russia by Communists. In the U.S. it was a political force only briefly but the Hay Market Riot and assassination of McKinley brought a law barring anarchists from the country. A leading American anarchist was Emma Goldman."

It wasn't exactly a cheeseburger deluxe custom-made to my taste but it sounded like there were possibilities. Abolition of the state seemed like a nice idea. Like Kropotkin, I would resist violence as part of the doctrine. But I would now be free to free associate. If I was a true anarchist, I would even resist following any of the doctrine of anarchists before me. Emma Goldman would be worth a look. She was, it turned out, busted for talking up birth control in 1916 and obstructing the draft in 1917. Now there was a lady after my own heart. If only Alex Bell had bothered to come up with a serviceable time machine.

I could see at once that there would be no point in trying

to establish a group of anarchists. The concept wreaked of hypocrisy. Besides, if independence of mind was paramount, how could any of us agree on anything? The abolition of the state, perhaps, but the means would be up for infinite discussion.

There was a well-known proponent of political anarchy ensconced in the Political Science department of a nearby university so I went to him for advice. Dr. Wallace turned out to be of some minimal use.

"How do you know the state is intrinsically evil?" I asked. I confess I didn't really know what "intrinsically" meant.

"Well, think of this. If man values his independence, his individuality, then to co-operate, to follow the will of another, or to bend to the will of say, ten thousand others, corrupts his individualism, his independence."

"I see what you mean. But how do you live in a country where there is no government, only anarchy?"

"Ah, yes. Well, you see, each man has his own freedoms, his own choice to do as he pleases as long as he harms no one else."

"But if he does . . . if another man, say, harms you or your family in some way, what do you do?"

"I simply shoot him."

Now it was beginning to be a bit clearer. "But in a true anarchy, there is no property, therefore no right to hold onto anything you own."

"Perhaps."

"Perhaps?"

"Well, yes, in theory. My house is your house. My wife, your wife. My food, your food." He laid a set of car keys on the desk. "You see those keys? They are to my car, my Saab. I will not give those car keys to you."

"But I thought you were an anarchist."

"I am. The state, however, is fundamentally evil and I live, to some degree, within the powers and jurisdiction of the state. I am obliged to follow many of its doctrines even though they go against my principles. Therefore, I maintain property and will protect it if need be."

"If I stole those keys and took your car, would you call the cops?"

"Absolutely."

"But not in an ideal anarchic society?"

"In an ideal anarchic society, I would not. But one will never exist, except in theory, so I will never have to worry about giving up my Saab to a young man like you."

"One more question. Do you pay taxes?"

"Yes," said Professor Wallace. "Are you crazy? I'd go to jail if I didn't."

"But your tax money goes to make war on other countries and to create more nuclear bombs that will probably destroy the earth."

He seemed unperturbed by all of this. "Of course, young man. Of course they do. It is because the state is intrinsically evil. Government of any form sucks." There was a long thoughtful pause. "But I have tenure and a pension to think of. I don't want to spend the rest of my life incarcerated with mobsters and sex offenders. An anarchist has to be realistic about these things."

"Thanks for your time."

"You're welcome. Oh yes, one more thing. Did you know that Christ was an anarchist?"

"I think I had a suspicion," I said and turned to go.

It was clear that political anarchy was suspect. However, personal, apolitical, and creative anarchy had possibilities. I was anxious to avoid getting political at all these days, so I was headed toward art. I was in a film-making phase — super 8 was the ticket. So, along with my girlfriend, I made a film that went like this:

A young man is sitting reading a book beneath a lamp. He has a small, real, but stuffed alligator by his side. He gets up and walks the alligator to a nearby stream and lets it go.

Later he finds a hurt butterfly caught on a rooftop TV antenna. He picks it up, shelters it from the cold winds, takes it home, then lets it go. That same day he finds a moose leg bone in an outdoor incinerator and he carries the bone around with him for a long time. Then there is a family photographic portrait that is waiting in a tree branch. In the end, he returns to the forest to retrieve the stuffed baby alligator that is going over a small waterfall. The film was called *Anchorage* and an Alaskan road sign, stolen and carried back to New Jersey, was used for the title.

When asked what the film meant, I would say it was a film about anarchy. It was a statement of sorts, a doctrine of creative anarchy that I hoped would change the way people looked at themselves, at the rift between conformity and non-conformity, about property and the intrinsic evil of the state.

Creative anarchy worked well for me for a while. Then people started thinking that I was not so much of an anarchist as I was simply a crazy person. When I discovered how much fun it was to be simply crazy, I went along with it. As a philosophy of living, it presents even fewer restrictions than creative anarchy.

6

More Than a Dog

F ourteen years is a long time for a dog to live. My dog, Jemima, has just died. She lived with us for fourteen years, and I feel like a major chapter in my life is over. I thought that I was getting more mature about my attitude towards death — it comes with the territory or being nearly forty. But I guess nothing has changed. I still want to stare death straight in the teeth, kick, bite, and bash at it and then drive it away, back into the cave of its origin. My dog died and suddenly the world is a cruel, pointless place full of horrible traps and broken promises.

I know others have sustained much worse than this, but all I have is me right now, sitting in a warm flood of October sunlight, holding my dead Jemima in my arms as her body grows slowly more stiff with rigor mortis.

This was the fall that I discovered the holes in some maple leaves. One day I noticed that the holes looked like cigarette burns. It was the same day my daughter brought home her grade three collection of poems all written by her class. These were the poems written by kids each year ever since autumn had a name. Poems about leaves falling, about the colors. My daughter's poem had a deep resonance of reincarnation in it . . . or so I can argue. Something about falling to the ground and being regenerated again next year as new leaves on the trees.

I was pretty sure that the cigarette holes in the maple leaves were from insects. So I didn't want to say too much. You start worrying about insect holes in leaves around here and pretty soon somebody is flying in at low altitudes lacing the land with billowing clouds of insecticide. I wanted to keep my mouth shut.

But then with the change of colors, I saw that *all* the leaves had holes in them. Pall Mall burns, Chesterfields, Tiperillos, and double stogey holes big enough to put your thumb and favorite finger through. I turn on David Suzuki one night and have to face up to the fact that it's acid rain. *No, you're kidding. Acid ain't exactly ACID*, I say to the TV. I mean, we're just talking about a high ph in the rain, not hydrochloric acid. But, *sorry*, the TV talks back, ACID as in ACID. And I'm looking at a 26-inch screen full of de-nuded sugar bush maple trees in Quebec. Ronald Reagan isn't even convinced yet that acid rain is a nuisance let alone a hazard, and already we've defoliated a fair proportion of La Belle Provence.

Maybe next year the butt burns in the maple leaves will get bigger, the year after that bigger still and finally, I'll wake up one spring and it will sink in. The leaves won't be back. Son of a gun.

Death always sneaks up on you and kicks you in the head, sometimes when you're trying to be a nice guy. I just thought I'd be a nice guy and take my family to see *Who Framed Roger Rabbit?* While we were gone, Jemima got into some household garbage and ate a wad of chicken fat that we humans did not want to eat. This set off some internal problems and she died two days later, after her heart began to fade. Death by chicken fat.

A dog will help you out through the roughest of times and, while mine was no Hollywood heroine, she was there when I needed her and she had been a constant all through that four-teen year span that saw me wrestle myself into manhood and familyhood. And I needed that.

She was the runt of a litter of puppies living at a house near the ocean in Seaforth. We had followed one of her sisters there to the house but the other dog disappeared and Jemima discovered us. She saw a meal-ticket and then some and would-n't let us leave until she was safe inside the old vw van. Part beagle, part Labrador, she was born stubborn and conniving and not particularly intelligent except when it came to things involving sustenance and loyalty.

It was a momentous summer. Terry and I were living in an old farm house in Cape Breton. We bought a hundred acres of cut-over land up there, then a run-down shack in West Chezzet-cook for future years. We adopted Jemima and then we got married in Halifax. On the way to Halifax, the van, as was its custom, broke down. The bolts that held the heads on the engine block loosened themselves and we lost compression. I didn't have time to remanufacture the engine just then and there because we were getting late for our appointment to get married. So we hitched a ride to the family court. And we took Jemima with us.

It was a classic hippie marriage. Terry and I were in torn blue jeans and flannel shirts. And Jemima, still a puppy, was held in my arms. All three of us were wedded together by a Halifax judge named Hudson. Judge Hudson had apparently seen it all and had no problems with the dog. He liked the idea. Jemima was well-behaved and didn't let go the floodgates of pee until we had nearly made it back out the door of the courthouse and into the streets.

Judge Hudson had asked if we wanted God in the cere-mony. This seemed like such an interesting philosophical question that I almost delayed the proceedings to give it a think through. Was I still deep-down a Christian, an agnostic, or a mere pessimist at that point about religion? I wasn't sure but I decided that, above all, I wanted to be tolerant and open, so of course we allowed God into the text. Next, Judge Hudson had pointed to an audience about to come in the door. "And would you mind if these visiting Dalhousie Law Students be admitted to observe?"

I could see that once God had his foot in the door, crowds of others would soon follow. Sure, why not? But the universe was unfolding and happiness leaked out all over the room like an overflowing bathtub.

Jemima was a survivor. She never got hit by a car but she did get her tubes tied at an early age. She also snapped a tendon in her back leg and couldn't walk until a vet lashed the tendon back together. Once she had her face ripped open by an Irish setter but it healed quickly after several stitches and a few weeks. A short while before she died, I had already killed her in a book. *December Six / The Halifax Solution* was my personal attempt to disarm the world. It began with a fictional scenario of myself and my family huddled in the basement while Halifax, eleven miles away, is leveled by a second December explosion, this time as part of a global nuclear war.

In the scenario, Jemima is left outside. She was off chasing a chipmunk. (She never, ever, actually caught one in her entire fourteen year career.) After the explosion, we hear her from the basement. She is undoubtedly burned and dosed lethally with radioactivity. She howls and cries but I, of course, cannot let her down in the basement with the family. I plot that, later, I'll have to go up and do her in lest she suffer and increase our agony as we all slowly die of radiation.

I know that sounds almost pointlessly gruesome, but I figure it's necessary for people to live through some of the grief before they will begin to do anything about the 60,000 nuclear weapons still lingering on the planet there in the bleak days of the Cold War.

Not everyone is brave enough to read my short little book but many who have say that they weren't moved by my portrait of my family in the basement, by the decimation of Halifax, and the death of a hundred thousand or so Nova Scotians (not to mention the millions of others worldwide). But what stuck in their imagination was my old beagle/Labrador dog scratching at what was left of the back door and how tragic her demise seemed.

So now, after she is gone, I begin to wonder. Just suppose it's that image of Jemima that sticks in the minds of enough people who have read the book. Dying humans are not nearly as moving as dying family dogs. Just suppose it is the image of Jemima that finds its way into the heads and hearts of people in power? The book has gone out to presidents, prime ministers, and other politicians. I want to just suppose it didn't end up in the trash can or in the files of the CIA. Maybe this is why she adopted us in Seaforth that snap-crackling crisp July morning.

December Six was not a fun book to write. In fact, it was a hard book to publish. I sent the manuscript everywhere and it was turned down over and over. Perhaps it was poorly written. Maybe it was so baldly naive that it embarrassed everyone who read it. I don't know. Many of the rejections sounded like this. "This is a good idea and your message needs to be heard. I just don't think we can market the book." If only disarmament books were as tantalizing and as easy to market as new weapons delivery systems, I thought.

Another answer. "We find that we can't get people to buy books about nuclear war because buyers find the subject matter too depressing." Hmm. If we avoid dealing with it because it is too depressing, then all hope is gone. The popularity of fondue cookbooks and the lives of the rich and famous will invariably insure megadeath by thermonuclear devastation.

So I published the book myself. And it worried the hell out of me. I had never done that before and I would be ridiculed. I sent the proofs back to the printer in Winnipeg for the final time and waited for the book with something less than anticipation.

Now, the day that the seventy odd boxes of books arrived
from Winnipeg a bird appeared. I had a small, argumentative
flock of six pigeons, and in the day they fly around a bit and
mostly sit on my new shingles and reduce the property value of
my house. But on the day the books arrived, this one lone, pure
white (except for one tiny trace of black in a tail feather) pigeon
arrives from out of the deep blue sky and lands on the roof with
my birds. He's small for a pigeon and if you saw him sitting by
the side of the road you'd probably think he was a white dove.
But when I see his arrival, having barely finished heaving all the
books into my office, I get a long string of goose bumps down
my spine. Somebody is trying to tell me something.

I know, I know. Big deal. A lost pigeon joins my bunch. So
what? Stray pigeons find new homes all the time. Well, after a
while, that was what I said. He went in with my birds at night
and they gave him a hard time. I've lectured them on the sins of
territoriality but it does little good. Still, the white pigeon stayed
on. I was busy promoting my book on radio and TV and I lost
interest in him. So one day, three weeks into his visitation, he
disappeared. And that was that.

Other problems developed among the pet community. My
daughter's budgie was flying around the house one night while
we were watching *Hooperman* on TV. He landed on a window
ledge and chipped away some ancient paint, swallowed it, and
got lead poisoning. Damn. The world is so fraught with such
peril that it's hard to figure out how any of us survive. I took
Chewy to a Halifax vet, a bird specialist. After a few days she said
Chewy was paralysed and on his way out but that she'd keep
giving him injections.

Then came Roger Rabbit, the chicken fat, and two days of
watching life fade.

On Jemima's last night, I slept on the floor with her. She
was having a hard time breathing and periodically threw up on
the floor until she had nothing left in her to get rid of. I lay
beside her and tried to keep her warm as she grew colder and

colder. She'd try to get up but I had to lay her back down over and over because she could no longer walk. I talked and sang to her and my eyes burned from midnight tears. By morning she was incapable of moving but the panting had stopped. I had a one-hour radio talk show scheduled to discuss disarmament and argue with callers about why Halifax should declare itself a nuclear weapons free zone.

Maybe I should have stayed with Jemima, but she was no longer in pain. I lay her on a cushion in a warm pool of sunlight and would return in an hour and a half. I was praying for a miracle but felt a sort of responsibility to go talk disarmament, believing that every public forum counted. It was a heavy rock station and I expected flack from pro-military freaks. It could be a vital eye opener for some few listeners who had never considered keeping American nuclear-armed subs out of Halifax Harbour. So I went and did the radio show.

Halifax Harbour was an amphitheatre of golden sunlight and blue sparkling water. From the top of Queens Tower in the Q104 studio you could see as far as the curve of the planet allowed. I put a cork in the bottle of emotion as only men can do. If I had cried and wallowed in self-pity half the way to Dartmouth, I was now a clear-headed rational, statistic-toting technician of pure argument and persuasion.

The hour passed. Mostly men phoned in arguing that we needed the jobs brought by visiting American subs and that we were, by tradition, a military town and that, alas, there was nothing we could do about the arms race. One mayoralty candidate called to say that we should be "not so negative about the military." We should be instead "cheerfully optimistic." I agreed. We needed to persuade the Canadian military of the problems inherent in nuclear war and that we did indeed have to exhibit a kind of cheerful optimism if we were to save ourselves.

And then I returned home. Jemima had faded and was now dead. I gathered her up in my arms and howled long and hard, alone at home with my dog and my sadness. I listened for a heartbeat for many minutes but knew that she was not there. Her fur was still warm. A black dog lying in the sun, dead or alive, is a solar sponge. I rocked us together until my heart unclenched and my eyes ached. Then I lay her down in the greenhouse and walked out into the beautiful blue sky day.

I looked out to sea, then turned around and looked up on my roof. The white bird had arrived again. The pure white pigeon was back. She had arrived at the very hour that Jemima died. My wailing stopped and turned to laughter as the bird flew down near my head and sat there looking puzzled and pleased all at once.

At noon I buried Jemima high up on the hill and cried some more as I shoveled the dirt over her for good. It was, of course, a job that I had to do myself and it was my last goodbye.

That evening, the white bird allowed me to pick it up. I brought him into the greenhouse and fed him by hand. I think that some religions suggest that animal souls transmigrate from one creature to the next, but it seemed unlikely that Jemima had been born again so quickly in a fully grown pigeon. But clearly, some line of communication had taken place in the animal kingdom, and my pain was relieved by this miniature white pigeon.

For whatever reasons, he had arrived as a signal of new life at the hour when death had swallowed up the great blue world.

The dog who would save the world was gone but this was yet a planet worthy of some trust. My daughter's budgie staged a miraculous recovery and returned two weeks later more full of life and chatter than I had ever seen it.

Sometimes I think I still hear Jemima bark. Sometimes I forget that she's not there to eat the crumbs off the floor. Sometimes I still think she's begging for meat scraps at the table. And sometimes I can't help thinking that a bird is just a little bit more than a bird or that a dog is somewhat more than a dog.

7

Death Comes to Stoney Beach

July 1 — Canada Day. I am lying down on my bed in the middle of the afternoon. Holidays always make me lethargic. The phone rings and I hear that someone is caught in the tidal current of the Lawrencetown River at Stoney Beach and she is being sucked to sea.

I jump in my car and drive to the nearby public beach, scream to the lifeguards to follow me to Stoney. I race on ahead, facts sorting themselves out in my brain. Seconds count. There are no lifeguards at Stoney even though the water is warmer there, and on this rare, warm summer day, it will be jammed with swimmers from Halifax and Dartmouth. At low tide, the river empties the lake into the sea with a strong, deep channel that comes too close to shore. It's not an undertow, just gravity racing inland waters back to the ocean.

I can't drive fast enough. Traffic is sluggish near the headland with drivers slowing down to look at the blue, clean ocean. I smash onto my horn and curse out the window. Finally, I clear the top of the hill and pull into the tea room parking lot, run to the edge of the high dirt cliff, and look down and out to sea. Nothing. Nearby, beneath me at Stoney Beach, everything looks normal. No one running, no one screaming. The sound of kids laughing lifts high in the air and finds me here, baffled, feeling startlingly alone. Something tells me not to assume too much.

Directly below me, on the loose stones and boulders near the tip of the headland sits a young man on a rock. He looks like he's been swimming. I jump the edge, wearing nothing on my feet but cheap rubber sandals, and slide the loose soil and scree to the shore's edge, a hundred feet down.

"Is there someone out there?" I ask, pointing out to sea. My heart is pounding. I'm already out of breath. The guy shakes his head. I see his pale, ghostly face. He's shivering and hugging his knees.

"I tried," he says to me, groping to find words.

But I'm half-hypnotized by the sound of people having fun so near. So hard to keep convincing myself it's a crisis.

"She's still out there," he says.

"Where?" I ask.

He points a finger. Weighty seconds pass. I can see that the river current snakes close to shore here before it loses it's strength and blends with the wide, open ocean. I follow its path with my eyes out to sea.

Then I see something. I see her. Face down.

I start running over the slippery rocks toward the victim. I fall several times, tearing my legs on sharp barnacles. My sandals fall off and I'm stumbling along in my socks. The water grows up toward my chest and I swim. I'm shocked at how warm it is. I was expecting ice as always. But it's the river sucking warm inland water out of the lake. The sea is so warm that I know that something is very wrong.

The swim is not far but it is enough to get me into water twenty or thirty feet deep. I lost my lungs long seconds ago on the way down the headland. Now I curse myself for being so stupidly out of shape. I'm gulping air and trying to keep my wits. But I've arrived. No flailing arms, no screams for help. Just an inert human form.

I'm turning over a woman about my age. She's rather heavy. Later I learn that drowning victims can consume vast quantities of water. I have her on her back now and I begin the struggle back to land, one arm looped across her chest. Some idiot voice in the back of my bedraggled skull bolsters me, shouts, "If you can pull this off you'll be a hero." Every Boy Scout's ultimate dream.

But I've had one quick look at her face. Blue-white skin. Eyes wide open. The water is still five feet deep when I let my feet find the bottom. I curl my toes to get a grip. While she floats on her back, I begin to give her mouth-to-mouth. Precious seconds.

My feet keep moving us shoreward. The impossible, slow weight that I felt while swimming now seems like nothing. She floats, I glide. I keep pumping air into her lungs. Keep trying to ignore what my senses tell me: the empty eyes, the coldness of this desperate kiss.

On the rocky shoreline now, a small knot of onlookers has appeared. The spell of holiday is breaking. Voiceless, lungless, I yell to them for help. For I've reached the shallows and her body is on the rocks. It has found the weight of all the sadness in the world. No one moves. A second plea but still none move. All the old tales are true. No one wants to get this close to tragedy. No one moves to help.

I'm alone on a stumble of kelp and barnacle-laden rocks, kneeling over a woman in a black bathing suit, breathing life back into her. *Trying* to breathe life back into her. The crowd further shoreward suddenly scares me more than anything yet. I feel absolutely and finally alone. Scared out of my wits. My only friend, my only ally is this woman, this stranger who so depends on me and me alone for salvation. I've scraped up my legs badly on the sharp rocks. They bleed bright blood. Even as I continue to breathe air into her mouth, I think about how foolish I must look here in my black socks, my short pants and T-shirt. I wonder if they think this is staged. "What is he doing out in the ocean in his socks?" someone might be wondering.

The seconds stretch out, each one longer than the next. It's at times like this I put in an order to God. *Don't do this to me, dammit,* I demand of Him. The tone is wrong. But I can barely think, barely breathe, and yet I must continue to administer more air to this helpless woman. *Please,* I repeat to Him. *I'll do anything.*

I am at the bargaining phase of a crisis. It has always worked before. Not a particularly religious person, I always believe in miracles. And miracles have been performed plentifully in my life. I have reason to expect one now more than ever.

The sky is indifferent; the face before me is lifeless and undemanding. I close my eyes and continue.

Shouts now from the shore. The lifeguards from the other side of the headland have found us. First to arrive is a girl, maybe nineteen, who has run the entire half-mile here. Together we begin to carry the swimmer shoreward, but even with two of us carrying the weight, we're too slow. Better to stay put and work at the resuscitation. She takes over the work as I gulp for air.

A few minutes later, other guards arrive. The first is relieved of breathing. Somebody vomits. Maybe the victim, maybe one of the lifeguards. I'm not sure which. Someone begins to pump on the chest.

"Has anyone called an ambulance?" I ask.

No one is sure. With more professional people at work here, I decide I should leave and check on the ambulance. I stumble off, over the idiot rocks. Someone in the crowd wants me to stop. He's asking me what happened. I want to curse at him, push him over. Instead, I run past the crowd and begin the ascent up the hill to the tea room, to a phone.

I have not felt such a burning in my chest since I was in high school and ran a mile after having had the flu. I pant and heave my way up the embankment. Cresting the hill, I am again in the parking lot. It's like I've entered another world. Tourists linger and look off to sea, kids play with frisbees. They look at me like I have just arrived from an alien land, a straggling Third World refugee. Inside, I call the ambulance.

Yes, they are on their way. I describe precisely where the woman is. I tell the dispatcher to radio to the ambulance that she is not breathing and her heart has stopped. The dispatcher answers in that classic matter-of-fact way that Nova Scotians sometimes have: "Oh yeah," as if I had just announced the weather forecast.

I decide I might be able to save some time if I drive down to Stoney Beach and try to commandeer a four-wheel drive of some sort to travel the rocky rubble to the point and retrieve her, get her closer to the road and ambulance access. I speed off down the hill. There are trucks and Broncos, and a fancy red Jeep but either the drivers aren't around or the owners refuse to get involved.

Finally I find a man in his twenties accompanying a blind girl into a truck cab.

"We need you to haul in a person who nearly drowned. Can you drive the shoreline?"

He says yes, then no, then maybe; then he says he has to leave, he has to get his sister home. Damn.

I race back up to the top of the hill and wait for the ambulance to arrive. When they get there, I lead the men down the hill. But I can see as we descend that she has not moved below. The guards are still giving CPR and mouth-to-mouth. But I begin to admit to myself what I have known all along.

The ambulance men reach her and go to work. Local rescue volunteers have arrived with a four-wheel drive truck as well. A crowd has gathered around the body now, and I fade back into it, then turn around and leave. I believe that if I don't stay around to hear the pronouncement that somehow a miracle can yet happen. It is a slow, painful drive home. The other beach is still crowded, but it's late in the day, and people are beginning to stream home on the road, back to the city, back to the end of their holiday. It will be off to work in the morning.

At home I tell the story to my wife. I refuse to admit that the woman is dead. Later, the RCMP phone, ask me to come file a report. I find out the inevitable. And I also learn the woman's name: Mary Lou. She was thirty-five and the mother of four kids, including a one-year-old. Another person on the scene said Mary Lou had gone into the water to help a child who had been caught in the same current but eventually made it to shore.

Human death in the personal, not the abstract, had finally caught up with me. At first I blamed myself — against all logic — that I should have arrived on the scene earlier. Had I driven faster, leaped down the hill sooner, spotted her an instant more quickly, things could have been different. It just wasn't fair. It never is . . . but this was my first real taste of the inexorable force that arrives on an average day and sucks the spirit from unsuspecting humanity. And at that moment, I fully believed that it was still *my* fault, that I had not done the job I set out to do. I often take on a sense of responsibility for things that others sluff off as impersonal. But this should not have happened to *me*.

Cruel, insensible actions, human or otherwise, strike me as purposeless and inexcusable. But hadn't I been living in a Disneyworld all my life, sheltered by good fortune, kind parents, and lucky stars? Who was writing this plot anyway? Didn't they know that stuff like this wasn't supposed to happen to me, a writer who believed in the efficacy of happy endings. It wasn't until nearly a year later that I honestly admitted to myself that had she still been alive, still struggling, and super-humanly strong in her desperation, she might have locked onto me and dragged me down too. I had learned basic lifesaving as a teenager but I was no expert. But for July 1 of 1984 and for the rest of that summer, it wasn't enough to say to myself that I should settle for the simple satisfaction of my own survival.

Rage and anger at the formulated laws of nature reached a psychic impasse and gave way to a sense of gloom and depression that I was capable of switching on and off at will. The sea, once my good friend and ally — the very reason I moved to Nova Scotia and lived by Lawrencetown Beach — had turned against me. It was not to be trusted. Society as a whole — represented in my mind's eye by those cow-eyed, impervious onlookers on the beach who refused to get involved — was benignly resolved to the notion that death was inevitable. One should not get involved in troubles that weren't your own. Or were people just plain chicken shit? Afraid to stand up to any of the death and destruction dealt out by government or nature?

I was only slightly amazed at my ability to turn off or on my inner torment. I was teaching a course that summer at Dalhousie University. There was much preparation, two hour lectures, and paper grading. Not once did I let my depression or anger intrude into the classroom. This I believe (whether it's healthy or dangerous camouflage) is a uniquely male skill that we learn quite young — the ability to throw the switch on strong emotions. It came in very handy that summer, allowing me to continue to earn my living, and get on with my writing.

Oddly enough, just before the drowning, I had begun what I believed to be my first really serious novel — a book about an old guy living alone on a headland on the Eastern Shore of Nova Scotia. His wife has just died. I call it a serious novel in the sense that, after a nearly a dozen books focusing on adolescent discovery, this was a book that would embrace a fictional lifetime. It was, as they say, about life and death. I wanted to write about death because I understood it so poorly. I was getting older and I wanted to unravel the mysteries as best I could.

But after the drowning, I found I couldn't get on with the planned book (eventually published as the *Second Season of Jonas MacPherson* in 1989). Death had come too close to me and I didn't want to rehash all the pain again on paper. Instead, I used my fiction as yet another male escape parachute. I wrote an entire novella that summer about two high-school buddies renting a house at a New Jersey shore town the summer before they go off to university. It wasn't about life and death at all. Instead, it was about sex and love and how easy it is for anyone at that age to muddle up his life.

It was really only a matter of days after the accidental drowning that I began to see where the real battle should be fought. It would be pointless to rail against death itself but there was another, closer, imminently confrontable enemy here.

There had been a long history of drownings and near-drownings at Stoney Beach which was now inside the newly developing provincial park. The water was warmer at Stoney. Parents would take their little kids there to swim in the shallows. Every once in a while someone ventured into the river current and got swept to sea. Lifeguards were too far away to do any good. Despite the recent drownings and the predictable crowds at Stoney, the government would do nothing to improve the situation. Someone else would drown there, possibly soon, if nothing was done.

My anger had a target. And I confess I felt a sense of new possibility. I was a warrior at heart and the idea of a good battle for a good cause — one skinny man against a fat and lethargic government — breathed life back into me. I took my case to TV, radio, newspapers and, of course, the government. My local member of the legislature, an energetic and dapper chap named Tom, heard my case, offered to take it straight to the provincial cabinet. I quickly garnered all the attention I could possible want from all the media. My optimism returned. What I was about to do was to save, without wetting a hair, the next, anonymous victim. What I wanted, simply, was a posting of lifeguards at Stoney Beach.

But deep down, I knew precisely what was going on. I was, at last, having my chance to outwit death itself. Maybe it's just because I've written so much damn poetry that I see everything as allegorical and metaphoric, I don't know. But it was clear in my heart that I was locked into a very personal struggle with demon death. If I could convince the government to give us lifeguards, I would have saved the next unwitting victim, cheated death of its reward. That's all I wanted. At least now I had a tangible means.

At first, things looked good. The media seemed to be on my side. In Nova Scotia, news of a single, holiday drowning is good for a lot of spilled ink and rolling videotape. (Later I would learn that the Stoney Beach drowning logged in as the 35th top story of the year in the province by a radio station that capitalized on human tragedies.) Tom promised to the cameras that something could and would be done. And soon.

I knew from scratch that I could not get into this wrangle with the government on polite terms. I went at it like a bull moose in rutting season. As the province grew sluggish in responding, waiting for the heat to lessen, I openly attacked the Department of Culture and Recreation for not guarding the beach. This was the same department that had, in the past, provided me with generous funding as a writer and a publisher. Clearly, I was nipping at the hand that feeds. And my teeth were razored sharp.

The Department's first round of defence against my demands for lifeguards was a plea that there were no extra funds earmarked to hire more guards. I immediately countered the argument by offering to the government, through the media, an immediate, interest free loan so that guards could be hired. I had figured out the salaries for a pair of lifeguards for the remaining months of the summer and it was not a fortune.

Their response: money now was not the problem. Cabinet was waiting for the official report on the drowning and the ongoing situation at Stoney. The report arrived at the very last minute on the day of the cabinet meeting. Tom had put forward my case to the premier and the other ministers. The story goes that most felt something could and should be done immediately. Unfortunately, when the report arrived from the lifeguards themselves, it concluded the beach was *too* dangerous. It should not be guarded. That was that. Government dug in its heels and had sided (as I saw it) with death.

A warning sign would be put up, instead. But the news struck me like a blow to the ribcage. I tracked down the report, found it inaccurate and boldly ignorant of the fact that Nova Scotians are notorious for ignoring any sign warning of hazardous currents. Hazardous currents of some sort exist at many beaches in Nova Scotia, but most people did not understand the nature of a river current at a beach site and they would continue to swim . . . and take their kids swimming . . . signs notwithstanding.

Tom apologized to me on the phone, but indicated the issue was closed. A sign would go up soon, but the province could not take responsibility for the safety of swimmers at Stoney. Walls were being built hastily in the bureaucracy to keep me at a distance. Spokesmen were being primed to distance themselves from me and create convincing arguments as to why I was wrong.

I spent hours on the phone arguing the invalidity of the report. The catch number was clearly 22. Stoney Beach was a dangerous beach; therefore, it should not have lifeguards. But it was dangerous because it did not have lifeguards. I argued over the next few months all of the alternatives I could think of: emergency phones, zodiacs, roped-off swimming areas, para-professionals whose only job would be to walk around warning people of the current and equipped with a walky talky to the guards on the other side of the hill. But it was all to no avail.

Once a government decides a thing at the cabinet level, it is virtually impossible to get it to reverse a decision. The sign was erected and the following weekend, as the sun sneaked out from behind the mists, I sat on the hillside and watched Stoney Beach fill up with sunbathers and swimmers until the parking lot was jammed tight. I phoned the papers and TV. More photos, more irate quotes from me, more footage.

The province had relegated the Battle of Stoney Beach to the Lifeguard Services (the folks who wrote the report), an organization run by the Red Cross. Great. I was in a daily battle with the Red Cross of Canada. Not easy to make them look like the enemy here. I was getting nowhere fast. I drew up a petition demanding lifeguards and garnered some three hundred signatures and addresses. I delivered it to my MLA, Tom, in Halifax, with TV lights blazing. His secretary, more than a little embarrassed, accepted the document and assured us it would receive attention.

Later, Tom's office said it had studied the document and undertaken a breakdown of the signers by geography. A certain percentage were from out of province (which was natural since many tourists used the beach), and many others were from outside the community (naturally, since most beachgoers are from the nearby cities). Somehow, it was argued that the document wasn't nearly as valid as it should be. Tom also pointed out to the media that while I was a well-meaning citizen, perhaps I was too "emotional." Emotions, he implied, were a sort of weakness in a man. Certainly, there was no weakness in anyone in government. What the hell.

Given the continued crowds at Stoney, and the presence of so many little kids swimming unattended, I was certain that someone was going to drown. What could I do on my own to keep that from happening if government was going to turn a blind eye to fact? I studied the river currents and tides carefully and it reinforced one of the few sensible points made in the lifeguard report: the tide was strongest and most dangerous near low tide as the river current emptied more quickly into the sea. I studied my tide charts and pinpointed the most dangerous days: any weekend day where the tide was low mid-to-late afternoon. Or any other particularly sunny day during the week when the tide configuration was the same.

I again asked for lifeguard co-operation — on just those specific times. But no luck.

The Battle of Stoney Beach continued. I was losing ground but not giving up. I took a letter and a copy of the petitions to the premier's office. I arrived unannounced but not irate. This was, after all, Nova Scotia, not New York. The premier would know who I was and might offer a meeting. But he was, alas, "not in." Instead, I met with an executive assistant, an older woman who reminded me all too much of the first really mean principal I ever had in school. She accepted my petitions, gave me a stern little lecture that I could not expect to simply barge in on the premier, and promised she would see that he read my documents.

I continued to phone every branch of government that I hoped could help. And week by week, I tried to keep the media interested in a new angle to this fiasco, but, in their eyes, I was becoming old news. So instead, on warm summer afternoons, I sat on the grassy slope of the headland during those critical hours, with my surfboard alongside, waiting for my second chance to do what I had failed to do the first time.

The summer ended. No one else had drowned. Rumors of near-accidents found me, but accidents that don't end in tragedy rarely get reported to the Mounties and are hard to verify. I continued to write letters, but I knew that I had lost. I was glad to see an end to that summer. I never admitted defeat. There was little comfort in knowing that my predictions would probably be right. Someone would drown there again. Time and tide would see to that. I would feel again when it happened that it would do so because I had failed in my battle against implacable forces: government and death.

The following summer, two women were swept to sea at Stoney. A friend of mine, a fellow surfer named Ronnie Ballem, was cruising out the river in his speed boat and heard the shouts. With his shipboard dog, Carlos, barking like mad, Ronnie and a friend hauled in the two victims and got them safely to shore. The media began phoning me again, wanting my two cents. But nothing new happened. The sign was up; that was enough, the government said. You can only protect the public so far (this from a politician who almost singlehandedly brought about seat belt legislation). But what about children? I countered.

Of course, the government had gone deaf. Maybe they had been deaf from the start. Policy was set and policy must rule over common sense as I should have learned years ago.

As my railings against the province diminished I eventually returned to my big novel. The old man, Jonas MacPherson, who had lost his wife, was locked in a spiritual battle with that elemental force that had stolen his lifelong companion, the woman he loved. It was a stronger, sadder book for my own experience.

One day, out of the blue, a man showed up at my office at the university. It was Len, the husband of Mary Lou. He needed to hear me tell him my account of that dreadful day and he had tracked me down. He was a Navy man; I was a long-time pacifist. We were unlikely friends but talked long and hard like brothers until both our anger subsided again to sadness and he left, thanking me for trying.

It took me thirty-five stubborn years to be taught that you can't change some things, that death, if not something worse, is just around the bend in the channel to lure you into deeper waters when you least expect it. Sometimes, I think, you have to just push on beyond the facts, knowing that you'll lose in the end anyway, and fight the good fight over and over again if need be until every last ounce of energy is drained from your body. Otherwise, it might be simply too damned hard for any of us to prove whether we are alive, after all, or not.

8

The Power of Darkness

I'm in favor of darkness. There's nothing I like better than a really dark night. So I recently found myself in one of those public battles aligning myself with others who were opposed to light. In truth, I was the guy who incited the protest against light. It seemed like the least I could do.

The crux of the battle was streetlights at night. I live beside a marsh at the foot of a lake near the ocean. East Lawrencetown is a refuge for migrating birds and emigrants from the city. It is a place of absolute, all-embracing light in the day and obsidian blackness at night. A cloudless night allows you to peer deep into space and travel dark light-years with your vision and imagination. Some nights the Milky Way is strung out like a whitewashed fence up there in the sky. You can go outside and dive deep into the darkness and feel the power of the great empty expanse well up inside of you.

Some nights there are so many damn stars you can't find Orion's belt loop or the Big Dipper. In recent years I've almost given up on finding Polaris. Each time I find it, I swear it's not where north is supposed to be. I think this is because my north is slightly different from true north or even magnetic north. But

I live in a world shaped more by my own interior landscape than by fact anyway.

Some nights the moon hangs low and pulsates an insanely bright yam-orange glow until it rises high enough in the sky to burn its way to silver. Midnight beneath a full moon around here sets the sea on fire and drives the sleep right out of you until you're staring bug-eyed out the window across the cold, platinum night landscape. On those nights we all go quietly nuts and wonder why our brain cells feel like poison ivy. Eventually the moon sets somewhere before dawn and we live drowsily through another day of half-consciousness waiting for a chance to nap behind an obscure periodical.

But then there are those clouded, starless, moonless, inky nights where you can't see your hand in front of your face. If the sea is sober and the wind is appeased, silence sings out the tune of the evening. Some nights a hellish glow remains off to the west where Halifax lies wrapped and civilized in neon, mercury, and argon lighting. People in cities are scared stiff of the night and try to turn their towns into rivers of street lights and glowing empty office towers that are lit up like bonfires. There's a primal fear that if the lights all go out, men will lose all control of their lusts and their greed and ravage the city.

And let's be honest; it is a fear of men. You don't walk down the streets of the city worrying too much about women. Not yet anyway. It's the men with their hearts of darkness. In contradiction to popular opinion, I think it's harder to commit a crime of violence without light. How can an attacker exactly see who he is attacking? Wouldn't he be cheating himself out of some special joy of the crime? I don't know, but then maybe that's because I think of darkness as a warm shield.

But this public fear of darkness was at the heart of the streetlight battle. It seems that a few of the neighbors worried about their wives driving a lonely stretch of highway along Lawrencetown Beach. Reports came in to the county councillors that women feared for their lives as they drove home along this mile-long stretch of empty expanse. It was the emptiness and the darkness that drove stakes into their hearts. If a car was to break down, the mythology stated, strange men would be waiting behind sand dunes ready to jump. All because there were no street lights.

Now I worried at first as I began to lobby the community for darkness if, in fact, I was trying to champion a cause against women. A county councillor had already persuaded a provincial minister to open his purse strings to the tune of twenty or more thousand dollars for streetlights. It was a mom and apple pie issue. A man just couldn't let his mother break down out there in all that emptiness and darkness. The night must be filled in with light.

Over a beer I lobbied another neighbor, a lawyer by trade, to join the forces of darkness. He agreed with me that we wanted to protect the night at all cost, that there were not strange men lurking in the dunes all that often, and that the logic of streetlights was perverse and wasteful. Other long desolate stretches all over Canada existed without streetlights. We wanted the shining sea, the back door Orion, and the gleaming lights of the far-off coastline. Hell, if you were to put in streetlights out here, you might as well move into some godforsaken place like Dartmouth and be done with it. He agreed with my position and was ready to throw his legal heart into the fray, drawing up dozens of word-processed letters in different typefaces and different color paper that we took around for signatures from anyone on our side.

It was mostly a battle of phone calls and letters, a merry irrational paper chase. I kept hearing of rumors of women further down the road in Three Fathom Harbour who also feared for their lives as they drove past the beach at night. There was something, it seemed, particularly sinister about Lawrencetown Beach at night. It's just an ocean and some sand dunes but people believed that it turned humans into werewolves or they feared that diabolical creatures lumbered up out

71

of the seaweed at night. It was simply too natural, too uncon-
trolled, too unlighted . . . and therefore, dangerous.

I was happy to learn, however, that it wasn't a male versus
female battle. Plenty of women signed our letters. Some agreed
that animals needed sleep at night, without the nuisance of
inert gas lighting. Almost everyone I spoke to was in favor of
joining the forces of darkness. We never could locate most of
the people who were haunted by the darkness along the beach.

So in the end, we won. While suburbanites were crying
long and hard into the night to their officials for streetlights, we
had successfully turned down an offer to urbanize the wilderness. The ducks could sleep now, the coastline could sparkle off
toward Cow Bay. Civilization would take one step backward. Our
enemies, no doubt, saw this as the first step toward the end of
civilization. Wild men would soon dig in behind the dunes and
wait for cars to break down. Plenty of country dwellers like me
would want to remove the power lines and telephone wires.
Cable TV would be a thing of the past. We'd be out there with
jack hammers tearing up the paved roads and blowing up the
bridges. Maybe this was only the start.

It was only a minor battle in the Dark War. The glory of the
Dark Ages was past. Our westerly horizon is already permanently awash with lights most nights unless the clouds hug low to the
ground. I think darkness has been given bad press for so long
that a public relations campaign is in order. A vast dark space is
healthy for the imagination. Bright light burns holes in the
retina of the eye and stabs sharp images into the brain. Darkness can be expansive and allow the imagination to roll freely
around in a brain socket as cavernous as the night sky. Darkness
is for dreaming. Bright lights fix us only on what is, not what
can be, and beyond the corona of light we still shudder at the
gray blinking perimeters. To travel in darkness is to trust instinct
over intellect and it seems that wisdom does not always grow
from the illuminated obvious.

Without the night-time shroud, the stars would disappear

from view. We'd remain fixed on the urbane clutter before our face. Trust the man who dreams away his night in a room swaddled in darkness over the one who dreams us into extinction inside florescent-lit bunkers where the sun or the stars never appear. May darkness continue to bring comfort and inspiration to us all.

9

Qualities of Mercy

There had been rumors of rats again in the attic for the past several nights: staccato bursts of sharp teeth digging through ancient post and beam construction at two a.m. Clawing noises in the walls near dawn reminded me of old Edgar Allan Poe stories of humans buried alive inside architecture. In the morning, a shaky trip to the attic would reveal electric wiring that had been snacked on. Droppings littered the attic floor like the spent bullets of terrorists. The rats were back again and something would have to be done.

We live in an old farmhouse on the edge of a marsh. The foundation is made of loose stone and the giant sills have been burrowed and bored through by insect and mammal for a couple of centuries. The entire wall structure of the house has provided major transportation arteries for wildlife in and out of our house for so long that I could never hope to close down all the highways. Even if I tried, new avenues would almost certainly open up. Wild creatures have attempted to move into my home with varying degrees of success ever since the place was built. What could I possibly hope to do about this age-old problem?

Mice were not so bad, really. They loved the greenhouse,

and usually did no damage. They ate a few leaves, left tiny, innocuous calling cards and left. When discovered, they could hop like kangaroos several feet into the air to safety. Once they had babies in the bag of peat moss. We treated them with tolerance until the babies grew up and discovered a back road into the pantry. They loved rice the best and chewed holes through every plastic bag of flour or cake mix available. My wife took to shouting at them loudly. They eventually got the hint they were not fully appreciated and moved into the swamp for the summer.

We had flying ants once — highly skilled carpenter ants that were determined to demolish our home in its entirety. Their gnawing in the night was so fearsome that I was provoked to call on a professional exterminator. The professional exterminator, however, turned out to be far more loathsome than the ants. The ants merely flew into the walls of the house, chewed off their wings, and proceeded to lunch on wood. The exterminator came with a tank truck of deadly chemicals. He sloshed the pesticide all over my driveway and nearly down into my well. He sprayed deadly toxins in my attic (where there were no signs of ants at all), and he drilled and sprayed until the house was unliveable for days.

"Don't worry," he said. "It's completely safe. They use this stuff in hospitals." Which explained why so many people were dying in such institutions.

"It's not 2–4–D or 2–4–5–T is it?"

"No. It's something new," he said. "Something perfectly harmless."

If it was perfectly harmless, I thought, it wouldn't kill the ants, now would it? He said he would come back for a second treatment in a week but I told him no. I paid his full amount and I was hoping I wouldn't have to hire something larger than him to free myself of the exterminator. Next time, I would welcome the giant flying ants with open arms and offer them two-by-fours for dinner.

We had a problem with moles once, too. The moles looked a little like the mice but they possessed a funky star-shaped nose and were almost completely blind. The sensitive nose explained their arrival at dinner time. The blindness explained why they would casually stroll up to the leg of the kitchen table and study the side of my running shoes with almost intellectual curiosity. These moles were slow and easily confused. They could never find their way back out through the woodwork interstate. My dog would playfully chase them until we opened the back door and used colorful language to speed them back outside where they would become intoxicated with bright sunlight and wander aimlessly until they would find soil soft enough to burrow back into the earth.

I couldn't help but like the moles. I could never hurt them. In fact, I never wanted to hurt anything that crawled or chewed its way into my home. Including the weasel.

In the dead of winter during our third year, a perfectly white weasel, as long as a yardstick was discovered by my wife. It was stretched out on our sofa in the middle of the day. The wife screamed. I came running but missed seeing it. The creature had siphoned itself through a hole the size of a Canadian dime near the base of a closet door. Gone. Never to appear again.

But late every summer, or early every fall, depending on what the *Farmer's Almanac* predicted for either, the rats would return.

Now, I don't suffer from any primal fear of rats. In fact, ours, I would argue, were country rats, not city rats. I had met up with one face to face in the attic once. Because of its size and shiny coat I almost thought it was a muskrat or groundhog. He bared two front teeth styled after gracefully curved scimitars. His eyes were obsidian black and he had a long black tail that looked like an old favored chainsaw file that I kept in a drawer downstairs. But he looked like a very clean rat. Almost sophisticated. I considered his origins, his breeding, and decided in fact he was just another one of God's creatures deserving to cross my path on occasion without meeting ill will. I would argue, on his behalf, that we should not bring an untimely end to his life.

That was until I woke up late one night and heard him, or his relative, chewing with great fervor through the ceiling tile directly above where I lay my head on the pillow. Any second I expected him to freefall into my face and ruin my ability to sleep peacefully for many years to come.

So I bought my first rat traps. And I killed three rats with that awful, absolute snapping-spring of human assertion until there were no more rats for that season. The first one I buried in a Sobeys shopping bag. The second and third simply went into rat heaven — the garbage can.

Then came the crisis late last summer. Our house was already full of creatures. My daughter had a pet hamster named Nibbles that she doted over. He slept much of his life away, curled up into a furry little sphere. On the odd occasion he'd escape and dash madly around the house like an ignited rocket until he found a dark impenetrable corner. Eventually he'd come out and be put back to bed.

But then came the rats again . . . or at least THE rat. I heard something one night rattling pots in the kitchen. This one had audacity, I thought. Something would have to be done.

I thought long and hard about killing a creature again. I didn't like the feel of it. There had to be an alternative. So I went into Canadian Tire and queried the counterman about all the potential devices for dealing with rats. I was introduced to newer, improved neck-breaking snap traps, a cornucopia of poisons that came in all the colors of the rainbow and in seventeen customized flavors. And I was even introduced to a staggering wall-rack of leg-hold traps, for when I showed the man the size of the rat I was stalking, he was staring at a pair of hands spread wide enough to embrace a bobcat.

But I was disgusted with it all . . . the gloom of deadly metal. "What about a be-be gun. You can pick them off and have some fun to boot," the Canadian Tire man said, luring me over toward the guns.

No, that wasn't what I had in mind. Reluctantly, he slinked off into the store room and came out with a metal cage called a Have-a-Heart trap. Son of a gun. He showed me how it worked.

You put some food inside on a little lever plate, set the door open, and wait for the rat to enter. When he touched the lever, the door would close. And you had your rat. Unharmed. I paid the man twenty-five bucks.

Now, ignore for the time being that rats plunder a fifth of the world's crops each year and that they are considered by many to be the most destructive mammals on the face of the earth. It eats forty-eight million tons of rice in Asia, alone. They carried Black Death in the fourteenth century and brought on the demise of twenty-five million people in three years. On top of that, rats are stupendous survivors — outliving even a hydrogen bomb test near a South Pacific island without any obvious side effects. Rats in cities had attacked people. (But, of course, mine was a country rat and of better lineage.) No, despite the bad press, I would treat my culprit with humanity, dignity, and compassion.

Later that first night, I heard a metal door snapping closed from the darkness of the attic. In the morning I crawled up with a flashlight and there he was. I kept telling myself that he was, in his own way, rather cute, even as he bashed away at the sides of the cage, flashed his brilliant teeth, and tried to grin me down with fiery malevolent eyes.

I drove him to the other side of the marsh, nearly a mile away, and set the cage on the ground. No one had instructed me as to how to safely let something go. I pried open the door with a long spruce branch and stood back. The rat sprang out, touched ground once, and jumped nearly five feet into the air, straight back into the weedy marsh from where it must have come. I drove home admiring my own quality of mercy.

Three nights later, I heard noises again. So the trap was

reset. In the morning, however, no rat had found his way into the safety of the Have-a-Heart heartland. And then, the following night at about 1 a.m., disaster struck. I was sound asleep but a rattle of cage metal and a single, feeble high squeal wrenched me to consciousness. It came from the back room where Nibbles lived in his cage. Damn! I shot out of bed naked, grabbed a flashlight, and ran to the room.

Now, I admit to having led a sheltered life. I simply wasn't ready for what I saw before me. The rat had opened the hamster cage and gone inside. He was standing upright on two legs baring his teeth. Poor little white Nibbles lay stone-stiff with blood at his neck. Never before in my life have I so automatically burst into tears. My wife was yelling for news from the darkness.

"It's the rat," I said. "I think he killed Nibbles." But I should have kept my mouth shut.

My eight-year-old daughter awoke and began wailing. This was probably the single most awful thing that had ever happened in her life. She loved her little hamster. Now she too had been yanked into the cold harsh night world of pointless death. What the hell was I going to do now?

I smashed down the door to the hamster cage, trapping the rat, but the rat let out an ear-piercing shrill siren shriek that drilled through my ears and into my brain. It pounded against the walls of the cage until it had actually broken the mechanisms that held it together. Maybe it was ready to lunge for my throat. I grabbed a towel and held the cage in place, even as the rat chewed at the metal and tried to grab onto my fingers. The flashlight had fallen and I was plunged into darkness. Now what?

My wife tried consoling my daughter, but the household was plunged into dark terror and mayhem. I did my best to hold the damn cage together lest the rat spring free and do God know what. My wife brought me some wire — little metal tie-things for plastic garbage bags. Eyes still springing tears, I tried to secure the walls and door of the cage so I could get the murderer out of the house.

It took me nearly twenty minutes to get the creature outside and into the car. All the while he bashed away at the bars with amazing strength, still letting go with grotesque, otherworldly noises that knifed the dark quiet night.

I got him into the trunk of my car and drove. What exactly would I do with him? I wasn't sure. I thought of just dropping him into the inlet from the bridge. Let him drown. To hell with the quality of mercy. I wanted revenge.

But something stopped me. Maybe it was the faint, impossible glimmer that Nibbles was still alive (for I couldn't possibly put my hand in to pick him up). Perhaps he was just in shock. Or maybe I was still reluctant to kill even this most vile of creatures on the face of the earth.

After a short drive, I found myself pulling up to an abandoned stretch of railroad tracks at a place called Three Fathom Harbour. Nothing around but forest, inlet, mud flats, and stars. I shivered in the cold damp air. I was still sniffling. I had brought a second flashlight but the batteries in that one too had lost the courage to go on under these circumstances. I stood with the rat and the victim hamster in the bright headlights of my car — an eery, awful moment that still haunts me.

I loosened some of the wire ties, opened the door. The rat leaped for the weeds and disappeared. I reached in for Nibbles and felt the stiff, near-weightless carcass in my hand, saw the bright red blood on the immaculate white fur. And let out a long, raspy scream that must have startled sleepers up and down this shore.

I don't think it was just the death of a hamster. For me it was a very real despair that the world did not always work as it should. It wasn't fair that Nibbles was dead. I had shown mercy to a rat and, in return, my family had been given this dreadful event.

Later that morning as I attempted to sleep, I tried to make

sense of it. Perhaps trying to make sense of a needless death, even the death of a hamster, is always a mistake. Had this been the mate of the first rat I let free? Or had it been the same rat? Had it found its way back across the marsh because the taste of hamster feed was too tempting to forget?

The morning arrived gray and dismal. A drizzly rain began to blow in from the east. Just to get out of the house, I drove back toward Three Fathom Harbour and I might not have noticed it if I hadn't been staring blankly at the pavement as I drove.

But there it was. A dead rat of the same monstrous proportions. It was square in the middle of the bridge crossing the inlet and had been run over by a car. It was halfway back to my house from where I had let it go free. I didn't have to get out of the car to give it a thorough examination. I could only keep on driving and stare at the beads of light summer rain that fell gently on my windshield from the heavens.

10
A Just Reward

A s a kid growing up in suburban New Jersey, I was haunt-
ed by the unshakeable stigma of being an upright, dependable,
good boy. I was the sort of teenager that parents actually liked.
No matter how hard I tried, I was driven by an unflagging
sense of duty to perform some manner of good deed. I was
also smitten with the vice of putting far too much energy into
my school work and getting respectable grades . . . an
affliction that would terminally alienate me from the fold of
punks and hoodlum girls who I longed to hang out with.

In the early years, my good behavior was awarded with a
long string of tiny medals given out by my church for good
attendance in Sunday School. I sat, Sunday after Sunday, in Mrs.
Lawrence's class, listening to her try to explain her way out of
the impossible questions asked by my more reckless colleagues.
Things like: if Jesus turned water into wine for the wedding, why
is drinking considered to be a sin? "The fact of the matter is,"
Mrs. Lawrence would answer, "that in those days, you couldn't
drink the water, so you could only drink wine . . . but it didn't
have any alcohol in it, of course." Jesus, then, was just trying to
help the wedding goers avoid dysentery. It wasn't because he

was as keen as the next man to party a little longer when the booze ran out.

Mrs. Lawrence took everything from the Bible in literal fashion. The world in seven days. (Of course, what the hell is a *day* anyway, if you don't have a sun or a solar system to begin with?) I had rational questions of doubt but always failed to ask them, preferring instead to sit quietly back and accumulate my attendance bars to hang from my suit jacket lapel. Oddly enough, Mrs. Lawrence never liked me. Her own two boys were incorrigible trouble makers and, even to her Christian way of thinking, there was something perverse about my persistent attendance and upright behavior. Had she known what I was thinking during her adamant lectures on the rewards of heaven and the punishments of hell, she might have comforted herself with the thought that I was not, after all, going to be let off the hook scot free and allowed directly into heaven after all. Instead, if thoughts counted as even one tenth the value of actions, I would be down in hell frying away in the fats just like her two incorrigible boys.

But despite all my best intentions of getting myself into some sort of tangible trouble whereby disappointing the entire congregation at the Palmyra Moravian Church and beginning a life of depravity, barbarism, and minor crime (like my other peers), I continued to chalk up brownie points with the church minister and several devout members of the choir. And even as I acquired favor in the eyes of the mothers of beautiful but unapproachable girls, I garnered total disinterest from their daughters and a kind of sullied wrath from my comrades who lived among the darker shades of moral existence.

Worst of all, perhaps, was the fact that my achievements were often documented in one of the local papers for all to see. The *Cinnaminson Era* had indiscriminately reported my good attendance record on the church news page. And then the *Triborough Record* photographer, Hank Whitkins, showed up at the school science fair when I was the only one of the winners present. I didn't come in first. I placed way down in honorable mention. That's the way it usually went. I've been a winner of second and third place awards ever since, an affliction that has followed me around like a baying bloodhound chained to my ankle all these years. Hank told me to stand in front of my three dimensional working model of an operational coal mine along with Mr. Stang, the principal, and pretend to explain how the damn thing worked. The picture was seen on the front page of the *Triborough Record* in every living room in town. When would I ever learn?

Other kids my age were out busting windows or spray-painting foul language onto cars in supermarket parking lots. But somehow I couldn't get the hang of it. I did my homework and always handed in book reports on time. My avowed hero was Glenn T. Seaborg, a world renowned chemist and nuclear scientist. In Miss Greenglow's English class, in fact, we were all asked to write an essay about one of our personal heroes. Other students wrote panegyrics on Mickey Mantle, Roger Maris, Paul McCartney, or maybe an astronaut or two. I wrote about Glenn T. Seaborg who had discovered a couple of new radioactive elements that existed for a millisecond in some cyclotron in a California laboratory. I was impressed by the fact that the man had filled in a couple of blank squares on the periodic table. Miss Greenglow, disbelieving that anyone my age could be in the vaguest way interested in such ephemera, gave me an F on the essay. She said that it was sick and disgusting to make such a mockery of her assignment. She said that no one my age would have written what I had. She sat me down and as her voice cracked under the emotional stress of the confrontation, insisted that I tell who my hero really was. "Who?" she demanded.

I pleaded that I hadn't been kidding about Glenn T. Seaborg. I, too, wanted to be a nuclear scientist and fill in new names of elements on the periodic table. Hadn't she seen my goddamn coal mine? I was a lover of rocks, of science, of the hard things of the intellect. But I didn't say that to her face.

She would have thrown me out of school for such talk. Instead I lied. I said that my hero was really Sonny Liston. Liston was a champion boxer who had recently been arrested for beating somebody up in a bar in North Jersey.

Miss Greenglow smiled sadly. "There. That wasn't so bad now was it?" She tore up my essay on Glenn T. Seaborg and asked me to go home and write "a real one." Knowing nothing about Sonny Liston, I spent the afternoon in the public library researching his life in *Sports Illustrated* and writing what I thought Miss Greenglow would appreciate. I was careful to throw in several misspelled words, a fused sentence, and two misplaced modifiers to keep her happy. I received a B+ in the end, replacing my F on the Seaborg essay because Miss Greenglow was a forgiving sort of teacher.

As the years swept by me, I tried to get the hang of things but still there would be problems. I was addicted to Boy Scouts, for example. While all around me Tenderfeet, First and Second Class Scouts gave up on the gentle regimentation of the troop and went off in the evenings to chase girls, smoke cigarettes, or start up gangs, I stayed on, first as a patrol leader, then as senior patrol leader. I wore those flamboyant neckerchiefs that my mother had ironed to perfection and that I had rolled and draped around my neck. The left pocket of my uniform was cluttered up with badges and medallions. I was encouraging younger Scouts to keep a written record of their good deeds and, as usual, I was setting a shining example. It was a tragic situation but there seemed to be nothing I could do about it but blunder ahead in the only way I knew how. I was awarded something called the God and Country Award for my acts of good citizenship.

I earned almost every merit badge in Boy Scouting, even a few that had been considered defunct for lack of interest for many years by the National Council — merit badges like corn farming, pigeon raising, orchid growing. I wore a long sash full of brightly embroidered badges devoted to specialized areas such as public safety, chemistry, public speaking, and journalism. (When I appeared at a formal function in full uniform, I was dressed something like a spurious dictator in a banana republic.) For the public safety merit badge, I remember having to sit at an intersection for twelve consecutive hours and document the number of traffic violations. I was a fastidious observer and record keeper. I counted several hundred moving violations. Over a hundred drivers failed to stop for the stop sign. Others were simply speeding, for I had devised a system based on Pythagorean principles to determine a car's speed. Schmidt's beer bottles were thrown at random intervals, some at me. Pedestrians were nearly run over, turn signals failed to be put into use, brake lights were out, and headlights didn't work. The clumsy carefreeness of human life swept past me there at the intersection of Church and Lenola Roads, and I documented every crucial detail of it. In the end, after tallying up the misdemeanors, I realized I was on to something. This was bigger than just a merit badge. I took my findings to the town police station. I stood before the dispatcher at his microphone and explained what I had discovered. I said that it was inexcusable and that something should be done. I showed the man with the drooping cigarette my Boy Scout I.D. card and my church membership card to let him know I was a person of credibility.

"You know what you are kid?" he said to me, after a brief interruption on the radio from a patrolman who reported that he was going into the Texaco station to use the can. "Kid," he said, "you're a little asshole. Now get out of here."

I thought long and hard about what he said. After that moment of police station satori, I eased off on merit badges but ended up becoming an Eagle Scout, the highest rank you can get, by just sort of coasting the rest of the way through on the merit badge momentum I had already built up. My final merit badge was a new one called mosquito control. This time around, town hall was on my side. The Cinnaminson Mosquito

Control Commission endorsed my work and sent me out around town with a long pole with a tiny pie plate attached to the end. My job was to dip it down into every storm sewer drain I could find and scoop up some water. If I saw any mosquito larvae, then I was to drop in one or two giant green jelly capsules that they supplied me with. The green jelly was a massive dose of some unnameable toxin that would kill off the little bastards before they had a chance to grow up and fly off to sting the mayor's wife on her backside during their Sunday barbecue.

It was the kind of task I felt well suited for. Eventually, Hank Witkins at the *Record* caught wind of my good deed and tracked me down one Tuesday afternoon for yet another front page shot. Once again, all the kids at school got to see just what sort of person I really was. It was smeared all over town in black and white. It was around that time that several of my best friends had launched into a career of stealing cartons of eggs from the rear loading bay of the supermarket and then heaving them at cars from overpasses. They just couldn't see the fun in killing mosquito larvae for the public good. And after a while of peer abuse neither could I.

Then came a watershed year when my Sunday school attendance began to slack off. I turned toward skateboarding and surfing and thinking about driving my own car. I bought a 1957 Chevy station wagon that I drove forward and backward in our small yard until I had dented in several fenders on the stalwart black locust trees. When I turned seventeen, I took my driver's test and passed. I had gas money because I still delivered newspapers on my bicycle after school.

And then the car began to change me. Without it, I probably would have sloughed my way into middle-age docility without ever getting into trouble. But since I had a car, and my buddies didn't, I was now welcomed into social arenas I had never imagined. I was up out of the sewer gutters of mosquito control. I was no longer documenting traffic crimes but committing moving violations . . . and getting away with it. It was a brave new world. My language was changing and my grades were slipping in school. It felt good, let me tell you.

I even began traveling on weekends with a buddy or two. We'd drive to exotic places like Philipsburg, New Jersey or Pocomoke, Maryland, for we were free and young and the highways opened up like promising asphalt conduits to the good life.

And then one steaming hot summer Sunday, we drove to a place called Indian Inlet in Delaware. It was a state park right on the coast with good waves for surfing. I parked my Chevy wagon along the road and we went to grab a few waves, my friend Roger Scarf and I. The water was crowded but warm and we argued with the other Delaware surfers about anything that came up. We stayed out in the ocean until we were sure our noses were so burnt that the skin would turn bright crimson and eventually crack and peel, maybe even bleed. Then we paddled ashore and headed back to the car.

Once over the dunes we saw that my car was about to be towed away by a tow truck. Three state troopers were overseeing the dirty work. We had parked in a no parking zone. Delaware, being the second smallest state, would not tolerate such an infringement without heavy penalty. So we ran quickly to try and save my car from impoundment.

Delaware State Troopers were swarming all around, their mirror sunglasses driving laser beams of light into your pupils any time they looked your way. I requested with great politeness and dignity that they not tow my car. But already it was being hoisted from the rear in an indescribably painful manner. My front bumper was kissing hot, sticky tarmac and I was getting frantic.

"Tough luck kid," the meanest State policeman in all of North America said to me and then sneered. I was royally pissed-off. (What would Glenn T. Seaborg have done at a moment like this?) The world was not a place of justice after all.

I was no longer a sash-toting, merit-badge-laden Eagle Scout, no longer an attendance award-winning Sunday schooler. I was one of the hordes. My car was being taken away. The world had a tight knuckle grip around my neck. Roger Scarf seemed quite incapable of grasping a way out of the situation. I was equally baffled. How were we going to get home to Jersey? How could we pay a fine? We only had enough gas money to maybe get home. We had hoped to stop at a diner and bum some change if the tank got low.

Rage was building inside me like a grass fire. This just wasn't supposed to happen to me. Yet another state trooper was driving by, at slow throttle. His face was cracked wide open. He was laughing at our despair. Then something welled up inside me, something I'd been wanting to say for years but hadn't had a chance. Two words — they were just there hiding out behind my tongue, ready to let go — waiting to fly out. I had just never been this angry before. And then the words liberated themselves from my mouth, urged on by my vocal cords: FUCK YOU! I said out loud.

The sound was almost visible in the air. Roger Scarf couldn't believe what he was hearing. His jaw hung down to his navel. The other surfers who had gathered around to share in the communal car-towing despair heard what I said and applauded. Time came to a halt. I might almost have reached out with my hands and grabbed onto those two words. I would have made a dive out into the hot sticky air, grabbed them with two hands, shoved them back into my mouth,and swallowed them. But it was too late. I saw them traveling into the window of the passing cop car. I saw them striking like a slap on the side of the trooper's head and diving into his ear. Holy shit, what had I done?

The car screeched to a halt. A mountain of a man got out and walked toward me. Mirror sunglasses signaled off toward the empty skies, sending out ominous news to the heavens. The trooper first turned to his comrades, a smirk on his face. He said something to them about me. I could hear the language, clear and loud. He was conveying his opinion about me. There was a string of twenty or so very obscene and evil words. I had never heard such profanity, and it was all concerning me. God, what had I done? Couldn't he see that I was just a skinny kid in cut-off shorts who had an excellent Sunday school attendance record? Why hadn't I brought along reference letters from my minister?

Too late for all that now. My past was behind me. The gravel crunched beneath his feet as he walked toward me, a massive bacon slab of a man, a veritable grizzly bear packed into a Delaware trooper's uniform, concealing his bear eyes with those empty mirrors that only reflected my eyes, my fear. I tried to remember everything I had ever learned while earning my "etiquette" merit badge.

He looked straight at me. The mirrors caught the sun and melted me to a pool of wasted wax. "What did you say, boy?" He had a voice like a jack hammer, jowls like two concrete blocks and the man was all strapped together with black leather belts. The smell was distinctly that of burning rawhide. What to do now?

I'd revert. Yes. Back to the old safe me. "What did you say, boy?" he repeated, his voice now like sticks of dynamite exploding in deep narrow canyons.

Honesty. Yes, wasn't that part of the Boy Scout law? A scout is trustworthy, loyal, honest . . . Yep, that would do it. "I said, 'Fuck you,' sir," quoting myself with utmost accuracy but not a hint of malevolence and I wanted to continue by saying, ". . . but I wasn't directing it specifically to you . . . I was just . . ."

But there was no time for footnotes. "That's what I thought you said, you little shit." And with that he shoved me toward the police car and, even though I was eighty percent naked, he asked me if I had any weapons on me — any *concealed* weapons? I told him I had none, that I had forgotten to bring any.

With that, he opened the door to his car and pushed me inside.

Along the road, I had become the center of attention. Fellow surfers were giving me the "right-on" fist-in-the-air sign. I waved back. They cheered and suddenly, as I sat proudly and indignantly upright there in the Delaware police cruiser, waiting for the trooper to finish cussing about me to his belted buddies, I realized I had finally done it. I was in trouble at long last. In trouble good. My peers out on the burning pavement and sand looked my way and smiled an appreciative smile. I had spoken for all of them. And now I was under arrest. They loved me. Finally, I had wrenched free from the old me.

As the trooper got behind the wheel and the radio crackled with messages of drowning victims and car thefts, we sped off toward the court house. Roger Scarf watched in penultimate amazement as the car departed. It was an epic afternoon.

I was taken to a courthouse in the town of Lewes where I was fingerprinted. "Isn't this a bit much for a parking violation?" I queried politely. The officiating clerk said that I wasn't charged with a parking violation, but with a section 242H, "a crime that's a felony in Delaware, son."

I was flabbergasted. Not only was this my very first crime, but I had already leapfrogged past misdemeanor right into a full-blown felony. I didn't know whether to laugh or cry. "What is a 242H? What's it called?" I asked. The clerk was having a hard time getting a clear print of my middle finger. It kept wanting to smudge.

"It don't have a name. It's just a number."

"Well, can I look it up in the law book or something?" I asked, the scholar in me returning briefly to worry the point home. I was anxious to see what my crime looked like in print.

"Kid, you think we show our law books to just anyone who steps through the door?"

"I guess not," I said, wimping out temporarily, overwhelmed by the magnitude of my high-numbered crime. Meanwhile, other parking violators were filing into the court house. They all recognized me and smiled with admiration. I sucked it all in as each one walked up to another clerk, paid a fine, and then backed off from the wicket.

Roger Scarf sat on a bench and looked bewildered beyond his usual limitations. At last, with the other lesser men of misdemeanor still milling around, waiting to see what would become of me, the clerk said I had to put up fifty dollars for bail, that I would have to stand trial because I had committed a felony. "Felonies aren't dealt with on weekends," he told me, "so you have to put up bail and come back Monday."

"I don't have fifty dollars," I said. "All I got is a five." I looked over at Roger, but he was already pulling his pockets inside out showing me he was broke as usual.

"You better find some money, real quick," the clerk said.

So I talked it over with Roger and together we began explaining the situation to the other surfers. I assumed it was hopeless. Fifty dollars might well have been five hundred . . . but miraculously, people began chipping in — dimes, quarters, dollars, ten dollar bills. I took down all their names and addresses and promised to pay back. Some just said keep it. They knew I had been crucified for their sins. I had said what they all had wanted to say. Before they all filed out, I had in my hands fifty-two bucks: the fine plus gas money. There was justice after all somewhere in the complex web of the world.

I paid my fine and left.

On Monday morning, from the pay phone at school, I called the Civil Liberties Union in Camden to see if they could help me out. I explained the nature of my crime and said that I had never been told what I was charged with or issued any statement of my rights. Isn't that how all the criminals on TV got out of going to jail for manslaughter or smuggling? "Sorry," the man said, "your crime isn't important enough for us to help you, even if it is a felony. Maybe if you had murdered someone or committed a rape, we could help out, but I'm afraid you're on your own."

Later that day, Roger and I split from school early. Roger had told everyone about my crime and my esteem at school had skyrocketed within hours. Girls looked at me differently. Several really tough hoods from my class slapped me on the back. I had suddenly become human, become one of them . . . and then gone on beyond humble egg-tossing and vandalism to make the cosmic leap to criminality as well. I breathed it all in like a rare, fine perfume.

I lined up someone else to do my paper route that day, and, as Roger and I drove back to Delaware, I explained to Scarf why he had to be there.

"You heard what that guy said about me, what he said *to* me. You heard his language. It was worse than mine," I explained.

"Well, yeah, but . . ."

"So I'll bring that up at the trial. If he called me those things, then I figure that we're about even. They can't bust me for doing the same thing he did."

"Well, maybe," Scarf said.

When we arrived at Lewes, I went first to the court house to ask again if I could look at their law books. I wanted to know the workings of my crime. The lady just looked at me like I was a mass murderer and told me she wouldn't let scum like me look at those law books if her life depended on it. I smiled politely and drove off to the nearest library. There, the sweetest librarian on the Eastern Seaboard asked me why I wanted to look at the law books. I explained about crime, number 242H. She smiled. "Isn't that a shame," she said. "Follow me." She was so helpful and compassionate that I was ready to fall in love, even though she was ten years my senior. We settled down to talk near the periodicals and she helped me locate my particular crime. Sure enough, there it was, tacked on to the end of the 200 section of laws dealing with civil misconduct.

Putting my hard-earned academic skills to the test, I read the law over and over and suddenly it dawned on me: I was being charged with assault and battery. According to 242H, swearing at a police officer was the same act in the eyes of the Delaware courts as hitting him over the head with a two by four or punching him with brass knuckles, battering him with a tire iron or stabbing him in some spot that would not cause immediate death or permanent impairment. I looked up at the librarian in disbelief. Roger Scarf looked down at the table and muttered, "They're going to put you away."

"That law must be unconstitutional," I said, not that I knew a damn thing about constitutionality.

But the librarian was quick to pick up on it. "You're right, it probably is, but people take swearing very seriously in Delaware." I guess it was because it was such a small state, there wasn't that much tolerance for profanity.

At the courthouse trial, my accuser was slow to show up. The judge apologized for the delay and went on to other criminal matters at hand: a goat who had devoured an entire garden from a neighbor, a traffic accident resulting from failing to stop at a stop light, and a vendor who had been selling ice cream cones at the beach without a license. Nothing but petty crime. Clearly, I was the criminal highlight of the day, but, according to the judge, the trooper who had not shown up was out searching for a lost child. Damn. How was I going to discredit his character and his morality now?

I squirmed and looked at Roger, who was more nervous than me. I was depending on his testimony. But he was doubting himself, doubting that he had heard anything at all. Maybe he was afraid we'd end up sharing a cell in some Delaware penitentiary.

Finally, the cop arrived. The girl had been found, safe and well. He testified. I had a chance to ask him questions like: "And exactly what did you say to your fellow patrolmen when you got out of your car and approached me?" All those years of watching my mother's favorite TV show, *Perry Mason*, were paying off.

"I said, 'I want to see what *our smart youth* wants.'" OUR SMART YOUTH! He had said nothing of the kind.

"That's not what he said," I told the judge.

And then I discovered that my captor had brought a witness and the other cop took the stand. Here was a man of the law, I was sure, that had not been within ten miles of the Sunday crime.

"Yes your honor," he said, "the exact words were, 'I want to see what our smart youth wants.'"

Shoot. I called Roger Scarf to the stand. "What exactly did you hear, Roger?"

But Roger, for whatever reasons, could not bring himself to use all twenty of the profane words that had so easily dripped from the trooper's mouth. I guess he figured that if he used the language, he too might get nailed to the cross. So, instead, Roger said he heard something but he wasn't sure what. (Hell, if I said one word on the highway, what would he receive for saying twenty in the courtroom?) I pushed on interrogating, trying to get him to tell the truth, but it was pointless.

Finally the judge asked me to take the stand. "What did you hear the patrolman say?"

So I blurted it out, the whole colorful string of profanity, word for word, just as I had heard it.

"You can stand down," the judge said.

I sat and waited in my pew. "You say you're innocent of the crime but that you used the words you are accused of?"

"Yes, your honor. I meant no disrespect by them . . . besides, the police officer just lied on the stand." I said this while both cops were still sitting in the room. Both *had* lied. Both knew it but they knew this was their justice system, not mine.

"The evidence seems to suggest the contrary. The Sergeant

is not on trial here. You are and you've already admitted, in your testimony, that you are guilty of 242H."

"Not exactly your honour . . ." but it was hopeless. He banged his gavel, said I was guilty but had already paid the fine which would not be returned. I owed $22.50 in court charges and was free to go. But I had read the law. "minimum fine of $50 *or* fifty days in jail."

"This has been a travesty of justice, your honor," I blurted out. It's quite possible I did not know what *travesty* meant, but it sounded good. "I'd prefer to go to jail," I said. Clearly I hadn't thought things through, but *my* honor had been tarnished. I was a man of principles.

"Do you know what jail is like?" he asked, more fatherly now.

"I've read books," I said.

"Have you?"

"Yes."

"No, I'm sorry the court will not send you to jail."

"I demand that you send me to jail. It's my right," I continued. Clearly, reason had retired for the day and my criminal ambition had taken over, my self-righteous indignation fanning the flames.

"Son, if you don't let this thing drop here, we'll charge you with contempt of the court as well."

"But that son of a bitch lied," I almost said out loud, but fortunately the blood had drained entirely from my brain. I was a cold white carcass and already, Roger Scarf, God save him, was hauling me out of the courtroom, getting my vocal chords out of range of law and order, truth and justice. He threw down a twenty and some change on the clerk's desk and hustled me out into the sunshine and into my car. I found myself completely speechless until we had crossed over the Delaware Memorial Bridge and were back in our home state of New Jersey.

Roger had to drive because I was so wrought up. When we were safe and sound in New Jersey, he muttered under his breath, "They're never gonna believe this in home room." And as I settled back into my seat, I knew that I would never be quite the same. Life was not as it had appeared to me, and if I was to survive in the world as it was, I might have to make a few minor changes in my expectations and my tactics. There were, after all, certain limitations in living by the Scout Law that I had never considered.

11

Coming of Age at Montauk

The year was 1969. I was seventeen and I drove a 1957 Chevy station wagon whose only flaw in its entire design was an automatic gear shift. My friends and I had surfed up and down the Jersey shore all summer on two foot slop. We needed better waves. We needed something new, something exotic.

Rumor had it that the waves were cracking like gunfire at Montauk Point on the easterly tip of Long Island. I remember Ed Kosinski going along. And Bob Bergstrom and Doug Stinson. They all threw in a couple of bucks and we vowed to run the toll booths of all the bridges in New York City to save on gas. Ed also suggested that we could pull into gas stations after closing time and drain left over gas from all the hoses. He had done this before and driven for days without having to spend a cent.

The truth was we didn't have much money. Most of us were saving for the fall, for college. But the road was calling. And the waves were waiting. And something was out there that our seventeen-year-old New Jersey brains figured was adventure, maybe trouble, maybe girls. Anything was possible.

Ed Kosinski offered to supply all the oil my leaky engine

needed. Ed's car, a 1958 Buick, burned or leaked a couple of quarts every fifteen minutes of driving time. Ed had given up on store-bought oil and, instead, purchased it in five gallon cans from the Esso station — used oil, drained from other people's crankcases. My car wasn't quite so hungry but I did let Ed throw in a couple of quarts of his recycled stuff.

And so we were off. It was early morning. Doug Stinson was still asleep, having forgotten to set his clock. We hauled him out of bed and threw his board on top of the car. Now there were four surfboards in all on top of my wagon. My straps weren't good. We all prayed that they wouldn't blow off on the Verrazano Bridge on our way to Staten Island. There were other worries: I noticed my brake pedal was mushy. I had to pump her a few times to make a clean stop. Ed argued it was all the more reason to run the tolls on the city bridges and the Long Island toll highways. Ed's advice was not always well grounded in reason, but we were trying to keep a close watch on our assets, so I ran a few, paid for a couple, and somehow saved us enough cash to suit everyone.

It was a long haul to Montauk, but when we got there we found some fine four-foot Atlantic tubes to ride. Then we ate some cold supper out of cans — Vienna sausages, if my memory serves me well. A quarter a can: one for each of us. Baked beans on the side and a can of Hires root beer apiece for a chaser. It was a meal designed to set off a veritable symphony of farts that entertained us on into the evening. In fact, we were all a bit tired and conversation concerning girls, surfboard wax, and New York drivers had dwindled to idle chatter. If we didn't have the farts to talk about, there would have been almost no useful dialogue at all.

Then came the problem of where to crash for the night. At the ripe old age of seventeen, the one thing to be avoided above all costs is a hassle. *Hassle* was one of the most overused words in our vocabulary in those days. ("Man, what a hassle!" "I meant to do it, Mom, but it was just too much of a hassle.")

But above all, you didn't want to be hassled by the cops. Especially New York state troopers or Montauk town cops. Police in those days were not nice people. I don't know how they got so mean, but we had heard from even the gentlest of our traveled colleagues that the only reason a cop was put on earth was to hassle kids. And we sure as heck didn't want any hassles.

"No Camping. $50 mandatory fine," the sign said at every dead end street, every dirt road or drainage ditch we came to. "Man, what hassle, " Bob Bergstrom would say. Bob would someday be a lawyer, someday even teach in law school. This trip was probably etching indelibly in his pre-legal brain something about the law. He'd specialize in every hassle-law that was in the book.

We certainly didn't have fifty dollars between us and what if the sign meant fifty dollars each? We dared not contemplate. But the idea of paying at the nearby, overpriced campground ("twenty dollars — Man you must be crazy. What a hassle!") seemed beyond our limits of tolerance.

So we drove around for hours on corrugated, potholed back roads out by some red dirt headlands. We expected they flew helicopters over at night to patrol for vagrant surfers like us. We knew the cops were hungry for our hide. They wanted the fifty bucks we didn't even have. All we wanted was a place to park, a place to sit in my dark car and fall asleep, sitting up if need be, without any disturbance from the law. But it was all too exposed. No trees. "No Camping" signs everywhere. "Yeah man, but is sitting in your car, asleep, like camping?" Bob asked, already in his young mind honing a keen, analytic spirit that would serve him well in a courtroom.

We entered into a lengthy dialogue over the legal definition of camping. It was probably premature in Bob Bergstrom's legal career to have accepted his learned opinion on the matter, but I was ready to accept his notion that if I kept my hands on the steering wheel all night, that yes, we'd be safe. If an arrest was to be attempted, we could argue that we were not camping;

we had just stopped to observe the scenery there at the butt-end of an eight-mile gullied, rutted laneway. We were nothing more than late night sightseers.

But still, Doug argued, we would get hauled into the police station and it would be an incredible hassle. So we drove on late into the night, wasting precious gas. Finally, on yet another laneway that made a snake-like path between what appeared to be a millionaire's mansion and the town dump, we found a pull-off so thoroughly canopied by some low, wind-swept trees that we knew this was home for the night, a place to sleep before heading off at the crack of dawn for some cold, steely Montauk waves.

I pulled my Chevy wagon up into the thicket until I had done serious damage to the paint on all sides of the car, then turned her off. There was no "No Camping" sign for the first time that evening. Bob Bergstrom argued that they couldn't arrest us because there was no sign. We'd lie through our teeth and say that we had no idea that camping was illegal in Montauk. We'd say that where we came from no one was ever hassled for camping or sleeping upright in their cars. In fact it was a common, nay, time honored practice down there in South Jersey, in the suburbs of Philadelphia. Bergstrom was fairly certain our false naivete would stand up in court. And clearly people had spent the night here before. The terrain was stockpiled with empty Schaeffer beer cans and broken Boone's Farm apple wine bottles.

The smell of farts in the car was so concentrated that, after a few attempts at sleep, Bob and Ed decide they would take their sleeping bags outside and sleep on the damp, litter-strewn ground. They'd take their chances on the broken bottles and the no camping laws. This meant that Doug and I could crash out in the car lengthwise and hope that the we weren't suffocated by methane.

Morning came and the battery was dead. We pushed the car out toward the highway in a slow, tortured morning daze and flagged down the first car that came by — a New York state trooper. I wanted to tell the guys to keep their mouths shut. Doug was famous for putting his foot in his mouth, Ed had carved himself a formidable reputation at school for defying authority, and Bob had a habit of trying to straighten out problem situations with a complex vocabulary that made no sense at all.

"Morning, boys. Trouble?"

"Yes, sir," I said. "Dead battery."

"You know there's no camping allowed around here."

"Oh? We didn't know that, constable," Bob said. "But certainly such an ordinance makes reasonable practice in such a pristine and nocturnally abundant place like this."

The cop, with good reason, pretended not to hear. "Whose car is this?"

I smiled.

"Licence?"

"Sure." I handed it over.

"Jersey, huh? I never heard of this town . . . what is it, Cinna . . . what??"

"Cinnaminson," I said. It means "sweet water" in Lenni Lenape. But the dude looked dubious. Clearly he believed I had made it up. He got on the horn to find out if I was wanted for bank robbery, first degree murder, or treason.

In the end, he gave us a jump. We cruised out to the bluff, parked illegally and went surfing. The water was cold and clear and the waves were good but New York surfers were very aggressive. Ed got a dinged board and people kept cutting Doug off of every wave he paddled for. We put up with the hassles, though, until our skin was puckered and we had all lost feeling in our arms and legs. To have quit sooner would have been admission that you were one chromosome short.

It was our last summer as surf buddies. High school was behind us. We were off to North Carolina, South Carolina, and Pennsylvania in the fall. We expected big discoveries in the few months left. Something more than waves. Something beyond the usual hassles.

Pizza Village was crowded but we had checked the prices in every shop in Montauk and it was the only one we could afford. We squeezed into a booth and ordered a massive plain cheese pizza and large waters.

Then this funny man walked over and asked if he could pull up a chair and sit at the end of our table. He pleaded that the entire restaurant was full and he just wanted a place to eat. "Sure, man," I said.

He asked who we are and what were we up to. Nice, polite guy. We explained that we were a bunch of no-good Jersey surfers and he smiled.

"What about you?" Doug asked. "Do you like surf or anything?" This was Doug's way of testing the guy, I guess.

"My name's Edward Albee," he said. "I'm a writer."

Doug looked disappointed. While the guy had not provided a direct answer, Doug assumed that the man didn't surf and therefore was of little consequence.

"Oh, like a newspaper reporter," Ed asked, picking up the slack. "You cover car accidents and stuff like that?"

"Not quite. I write plays. I'm a playwright."

At first everyone was pretty baffled. Dialogue had folded up shop and gone home. How the hell were we supposed to carry on a conversation about plays?

"You're not the guy who wrote, *Who's Afraid of Vivian Wolf?*" I asked. I was the literate one. I read books, even some that weren't assigned in school.

"Yeah," he said. His face brightened as the pizza arrived. "But it's *Who's Afraid of Virginia Woolf?*"

"I read that," I said. It had been recommended to me because it had a lot of swear words and some curious references to sex. I had read it all the way through and found the characters to be almost as annoying as Liz Taylor and Richard Burton who would one day play the two characters in the movie version.

Edward Albee was biting into a large pepperoni sandwich and I could tell that he was rather pleased to have discovered himself among the literati.

"Doesn't that make you fart a lot?" Ed asked, pointing toward Albee's pepperoni sandwich. From Ed it was an honest question. And so much of our conversation on the trip had focused on farting and hassles that it seemed only natural to him to make Albee feel at home with us.

"I hadn't noticed," Albee said. "But I'll be sure to give you a report."

"Do you make a lot of money?" Doug asked. "From plays?"

"Some."

"Would you, like bail us out if we get busted for camping around here?" he asked further.

"I don't know. But here's my phone number. Call if you get in trouble. They know me around here."

It was a generous move. None of us knew if it was his actual phone number.

"Maybe we could camp like in your backyard or something," Ed said.

Albee shrugged, neither yes nor no. I was thinking about the man and his wife in the play. They fought a lot and were just about the two nastiest people on the planet. I wasn't sure I wanted to spend the night in Edward Albee's backyard.

Suddenly Bergstrom lit up like a cherry bomb. "Wait a minute, I read one of your plays too — *Rhinoceros*." Then he went on to explain the entire plot just to prove that he wasn't lying.

The pizza was long gone by the time he finished. "Sorry, Albee said. "That was Ionesco. I did have one called *Zoo Story*, though."

"Oh yeah? " Bob said.

Albee wished us all well and left. Later when I got back home, I looked him up in *Who's Who* and discovered that he was a rather high falutin writer according to some. I tracked down a review in the *New York Times* and discovered that, according to the reviewer, the man and wife in the play weren't man and wife at all . . . but that the play was about two men, one in drag, in a homosexual relationship. I decided the reviewer had jumped to a hasty a conclusion and that Liz Taylor would never have taken the role if she thought that she was playing a man wearing a dress.

We never did get busted for illegal camping in Montauk. That night, we chickened out and stayed at the private campground. It was after the weekend and only cost $15 instead of $20. There we met some New York surfers who said *fuck* after every word and spit a lot. I remember the kahuna of the group introducing his boys:

"That's Weed. Weed don't look so good because he keeps getting his teeth knocked out . . . and over there's Killer, who does most of the knocking out of teeth . . . and this is Beggar who sleeps with chickens . . . and that's Slimy. Slimy don't care about nothing at all."

To that comment, Slimy smiled at us, threw his surfboard down on a rock and stomped on it. Pure nihilism. Heavy.

"See what I mean. Slimy don't care about nothing." The kahuna went over to Slimy's board, tromped on it himself and broke it in half. Slimy just smiled.

Instinct told us to keep the hell out of the way of these guys. Even to our warped mentality, busted teeth and being as carefree as Slimy didn't seem like a good time.

We met some other New York surfers, however, who happened to be renting a house nearby. They invited us over for a party. Life was looking up. At the party, the music was loud and the TV was louder. I hadn't thought much about politics for a while and here it was the night of the presidential Democratic convention in Chicago. There were riots in the streets, chaos on the floor of the convention. Somebody kept shoving Dan Rather around.

I had a slow evening at first, talking about surfing spots up and down the East Coast. Somehow, though, I suddenly found myself talking to a girl who introduced herself as Mercedes Quan. The impossible name still sticks in my head like a mantra. She was beautiful and Oriental and we talked about, of all things, poetry. All night, apparently she had been looking for someone to talk to about poetry. She was first year in university. I didn't tell I her I had just graduated high school. Instead, I talked about John Donne and, for the first time in a long while, realized that my entire high school career of learning was not a complete waste. Aside from talking theater with Albee, it was also the first conversation that I had on the trip that wasn't about girls, surfing, farts or hassles.

Mercedes asked me if I wanted to go outside and look at the ring she had seen around the moon. "A-okay," I said with a thumbs up. And that's where we were standing when someone in the house yelled that the sofa was on fire. Two guys in cut-offs carried the burning couch outside and the next thing I knew, Mercedes and I were overwhelmed by the awful pungent odor of burning rayon and foam rubber as the dark, acrid smoke curled up toward the halo around the moon.

The house smelled too awful from the fire, so somebody plugged in an extension cord and brought the TV outside. Mercedes Quan and I looked at the screen and together we saw the violence of the Chicago streets, the cops clubbing the students, and then the image of the CBS reporter, Dan Rather, getting beat around by a Democratic Party security guard.

Mercedes looked at me and said, "Something's changing. The world will never be the same."

She was so beautiful in the moonlight and so sophisticated that I was afraid to ask what she meant or say too much of anything lest I reveal my own political naivete. I fumbled for my car keys in my pocket. I was about to ask her the classic question,

"Would you like to go for a ride in my car?" But when I looked
away from the chaos on TV, Mercedes was gone. No one knew
where. I looked up at the ring around the moon, sniffing the
still-smouldering sofa and listening to the shouting mobs on TV.
At that moment, I wasn't sure whether I'd ever be able to go
home again. I don't know what I felt but it was knowledge and
loneliness and wisdom and pain all together.

My car actually started the next day as we began our trip
back home. But by the time we reached South Hampton, I
discovered my brakes were shot. If I pumped the pedal twelve
times, I could build enough pressure in the brakelines to stop.
Nobody in the car seemed troubled. Ed Kosinski said it was a
good thing that the car was a four door — that way we could
all stick our feet out and drag them on the highway if we had
to stop. It never occurred to me to stop somewhere and have
them looked at. Instead, I discovered that I could slow down
by downshifting the automatic into first. Then I'd use the
hand brake at the last minute for a final stop. But my prime
policy was to avoid stopping. We'd drive around slow cars in
the passing lane or on the shoulder if need be and wouldn't
stop for a red light until it was good and red.

We made one last side trip to Bay Head, along the coast in
North Jersey, not far from Asbury Park. While surfing, I
slipped on my board and fell chin-first onto it, splitting open
the skin in a neat boxer's punch-cut that dripped blood on my
white Levis all the way home.

While we were surfing in Bay Head, some locals broke off
my antenna to get back at Ed Kosinski who had crashed his
board into somebody while on a wave. I stuck a trusty coat
hanger in the hole and the radio worked fine as ever. I never
did get it fixed and that coat hanger was still pulling in South
Philly radio stations right up to the time that somebody stole
my old Chevy right out from under my nose in the Moorestown
Mall parking lot while I was watching Stanley Kubrick's *2001: A
Space Odyssey* at the movie theater. While the thief was outside

hot-wiring my first and most cherished automobile of all time, I was sitting in a dark room full of strangers traveling to Io, one of the moons of Jupiter, and feeling a little lonely and a little confused and wondering when everything would start making sense to me again.

12

A Hitchhiker's Guide to Human Kindness

It's ten thirty on a brittle morning in March. It should have been warmer according to my flawed prediction, but the wind is still scraping lustily off of the polar caps and knifing away at my ankles. I'm standing on U.S. Interstate 81 in the southwestern corner of Virginia beneath a green and silver sign that reads, "Pulaski — 5, Bristol — 30." My thumb is hanging over the pavement: ludicrous, blue, frozen into place like an icy wind vane pointing south. I'm hitchhiking from New Jersey to Mexico and, at this particular moment, I find myself pleasantly self-martyred by the fact that humanity, at least that segment which is now whipping by me in their respective Chevy Novas and Dodge Coronets, has decided to pretend I don't exist.

Last night I slept over in a house of some "Jesus people" in Roanoke. They had given me an early evening lift, and turned out to be genuinely kind and gentle folk. But they also felt obliged to load me down with personal salvation stories which, after the third confession, all began to sound alike. Apparently every last one had been a fairly successful drug dealer before

111

having religious encounters which prompted them to dump their goods in the nearest garbage can. Because I was cold and (yes) lonely, I went along to their Pentecostal church for evening services. It scared the living daylights out of me at first but I eventually grew numb to the imaginary languages and the epileptic contortions all around me by establishing a silent internal chant with the lyrics of "Help Me, Rhonda."

After the service, however, the ex-drug dealers calmed right down and, as promised, stopped hassling me about salvation and let me sleep for the night in an empty room at their house. My bed was an impromptu affair made up of a foam cushion over top of several hundred old hymnals.

I was hitchhiking to Mexico because I needed to break out of some ruts. I also wanted to re-endorse my shaken faith in humanity. I was succeeding at the first (even though I only had a long weekend in which to complete the trek before I had to start back to college). For the latter, I'm not so sure. I was, however, developing faith in my ability to master the unpredictable cosmos of the road.

Further down in Tennessee, I latched onto a truck driver going to Tulsa. Joe was an easy-going diesel driver who had a strong southern accent and a speech defect. He rambled on to me about his life, over the din of the Cummins engine all the way to Oklahoma. I tried but I never understood more than the basics of what he had to say. I wanted to be polite and invented stock phrases to respond. At one stop he showed me his load — about a thousand airplane seats. I had to hide in the sleeper at weigh stations and when we entered the airplane factory in Tulsa. Truckers can get screwed by their insurance companies if they are caught with hitchhikers. And insurance detectives, it was rumored, could be anywhere laying in wait.

My heyday was nearly a decade before this when I was going to college in North Carolina and in love with a girl in New Jersey. I faithfully hitched rides from South to North and back every weekend. I was broke and it was the only way to do it. I used a sign, I looked earnest, kind, and harmless. It took about twelve hours each way and it was a dependable, interesting way to get around. There were businessmen, retired colonels, jockeys, waitresses, priests, and other college kids who picked me up. Jan Murray, the comedian, picked me up once at the southern Virginia state line. The first thing he said was, "You're not gonna knife me now are you kid?" I assured him I wasn't and he told me lousy jokes all the way to Camden. He told me about his family and bought me a Slurpee in Maryland. Like most people who pick up long distance hitchhikers, he wanted some company.

The use of a sign insured the world that I was a legitimate person with a destination. I never made a point of dressing neatly for the trip, although other hitchers swear by the Brooks Brothers suit to insure that they ride in "good cars."

I heard stories and learned to be a great listener, asking all the proper questions. This was a way of paying back for the ride. There was the marine sergeant fresh back from Vietnam who gave me the name and description of every hooker in Saigon. There was the Atlanta lawyer who had just left his wife and was headed to New York "where they really know how to live." There were truck drivers who bitched about road taxes, congressional aids who complained about salaries. I heard more lectures and philosophic raps than I had ever encountered in college.

But then it began to lose its romance and I started taking the bus on the southward leg to D.C. and thumbing from there. Southerners were easier to attract than Northerners.

I was still going back and forth to the North Carolina coast from my school in Greenville as well, thumbing with my surfboard. I *believed* that people would pick me up and they did. But again my naivete and idealism waned and along came a few bummers. The occasional can of Pabst Blue Ribbon caught me in the ribs. I received a few warnings from the local militia to leave town and never return and then one afternoon in Raleigh a drunk picked me up. I made the mistake of letting him carry on about how he detested Republicans. He got so wrapped up in it that he forgot about driving and we careened off the road, luckily coming to rest against an embankment.

Then there was the Europe trip, thanks to the $165 Icelandic fare. There were very few roads, let alone cars to be found outside of Rejkavik in January and in town, buses would stop for me instead of cars. The thumb had a different meaning. In England, however, rides were easy enough once I got stationed on the correct side of the road.

And then a funny thing happened. I was hitching my way down to Africa from Brussels and after two days I had only made it to the outskirts of town — thanks to my own feet. No Europeans would pick me up and it was raining constantly. Finally, some American kids with a van adopted me and I stayed with them until I had spent all my meagre savings on gasoline. We picked up more hitchhikers along the way, both American and European. Many of the older locals who we picked up were rather scared of us. Language was a problem as well. One memorable conversation with a Portuguese farmer went like this:

Me: "We are going to the Spanish border, do you want to ride that far?"

Farmer: "Ah, Spain. My pants were made in Spain." He showed me the quality of the stitch.

After my friends sold their van in Cadiz and I was on my own, I had no luck with catching a ride from the hoard of Fiats and two-cylinder Citroens that buzzed by. I settled for interminable train rides through southern Spain and up to Luxembourg. Moral: when hitchhiking in Europe, be sure to take along some Americans with cars to pick you up.

Well, I finally had to get it out of my system one more time, and so one day I simply had to get on the road and hitchhike from Jersey to Mexico, which is where I began this story. The trucker gave me a few more miles down to Fort Worth where his family was waiting. I had finally learned to understand his language and found that as an independent hauler he had a routine down whereby he'd hit all four corners of the country in one circuit before returning to his family in Texas. He bounced his kidneys over about 12,000 miles in a trip, drank and pissed black coffee and every time he saw his family it was like he had stepped out of a time warp . . . and he was as happy as a fly on a turd. To me, this was education and one of the reasons I was hitchhiking. For the time being, I was on the high side.

I got let off out in the prairie where the Interstate took a fork and I headed on to Dallas where I hoped to crash for the night at SMU. I bumped into a fellow vagrant who offered me half of a hoagie which he had just bummed from a delicatessen owner. He explained that all of us free souls out on the roads were part of a fluid community and that we needed to stick together. This guy literally lived on the road. Like the trucker, he simply bounced off the borders like a silver sphere in a pinball machine. He hitchhiked perpetually. We spent a few hours huddled by the steam outlet of a laundromat to keep warm and I plied him for the lowdown. "You see, man," he finally concluded, "it's like an acid trip. When it's good, it's great. When it gets bad, it gets really bad." And we parted, he off to some relative in the Ozarks and me to Dallas.

A pick-up truckster got me moving into town and then he offered me a few hours work — he had to load some parts from an earth mover that he was going to repair. Sounded reasonable to me. But the sun was going down and when we got to the construction site, he told me to keep quiet so as not to get the guard dog barking — but he assured me everything was cool. Finally, some rent-a-cop showed up while we were hoisting the fender of a bulldozer onto the bed of the Chevy. He had the dog with him and was shining a flashlight in our eyes. I was left holding up the rear end of this outlandish object while the men talked. After that I never did find out what happened, but we had to unload the parts and leave. The guy paid me a buck fifty and left me on the freeway in the middle of Dallas. I was pissed-off and decided to keep to my usual routines and not worry about making money.

Everybody was going seventy-five on the freeway and no chance of a ride. So I went down to a gas station to find out where the SMU dorms were. An amateur gas station addict was just pulling his '61 Thunderbird out of the garage where he had just plugged a hole in his tire. He offered to drop me off across town at the university. Unfortunately, his skill at repairs was nil and at the first light we heard a loud hiss. "No sweat," he tells me, "I'll get out there and home in no time." It was about eleven at night and no air to be had. So he guns it through town, punching through a dozen red lights and squealing around corners. On one dingy street, he says, "Dig it man, there's the building that Oswald fired from." He almost seemed proud that it happened there in his hometown.

The jock who put me up for the night at SMU told me that if I made it to Nuevo Laredo (my destination) and I didn't have any jack, I'd probably get rolled and knifed and thrown in jail (if I was lucky). He convinced me that border towns had very little to do with Mexico anyway: they were outposts of crime and tourism with nothing in between. I was up for advice so I turned my thumb north again.

Outside of Dallas, a forty-year-old army captain just back from Nam picked me up. He had a sixteen ounce can of Budweiser propped between his legs and a full cooler in the back. It was eight o'clock in the morning. He refilled that cooler three times between East Texas and Alabama. It became an intense encounter session as we coasted though the heart-lands of the deep South. But something very odd happened. He started out friendly and jovial but as the miles and beers progressed he became enveloped in anger: anger over the hunk of shrapnel in his back, anger over his men who had been killed, anger toward the rednecks pumping gas ("who had balloons for brains," as he put it), and anger over the way the country was run. By the time I got off at a truck stop in Birmingham, I was mentally wrecked.

By 1978 it seemed that the road was no longer a friendly place. Hitchhikers that *I* picked up while driving my old beat up vw all inexcusably ignored the first law of hitchhiking. They were the silent, sullen types who acted like I owed them the ride. They made little attempt at conversation and when they did it was all about fights in bar rooms in Paterson, New Jersey or how screwed up the world is. One guy got pissed off at me because my radio didn't work and another character kept harassing me about loose change. It wasn't the cosy road scene I had remembered.

I remember one young lady I picked up as she was thumbing down Route 80 west of New York City. Here was a real pro. She was commuting between two communes, one in Berkeley and one in Vermont, where she lived intermittently during the year. She was reasonably friendly but nervous as hell — no way for a veteran to act. I asked what was wrong. It was the bumper sticker I had, one that had come with the car when I bought it. One of those big yellow things that read: SUPPORT STATE POLICE. I explained that I had tried to take the damn thing off but found that it was covering a big rust hole. The previous owner also told me it was good for warding off the Mounties and damn if it didn't work. The hitchhiker relaxed a bit and I asked her about her traveling experiences. She rattled on about truck drivers and truck stops and rich men in Mercedes but punctuated every scene with her fear of getting busted for hitchhiking. She feared cops of all colors and sizes. (Hitchhiking is still illegal in most places, in case I forgot to mention it.) She gave me the rundown on how Oklahoma troopers were worse than Pennsy cops but that, oddly enough, California "pigs" (she was still clinging to that idiom, God love her) were the worst. She claimed to love hitchhiking, but I don't think she enjoyed a minute of it. There was a lot of heat out on the Interstate that day (what with the new quota and all) and she literally trembled every time their white stallions came into view. Somehow, her extreme anxiety destroyed her ability to get much positive out of hitchhiking. She had a few good stories to tell though and, like most road addicts, she was writing a book on her experiences.

I tried to figure out what had changed since my own days of bumming rides. I began to pick up fewer and fewer hitch-hikers. And then one day it dawned on me that I really enjoyed the privacy and isolation of my own car with nobody in it but me driving predictably to my own destination. I turned to look away from a skinny long-haired kid by the side of the road with his thumb out. I wanted to avoid eye-contact. And it wasn't until I was a good five miles further down the road that I figured out who I had become. I was now in league with all those other drivers on the road back then, the ones I never had a chance to meet because they had turned away without giving me even an honest once-over. A sadness settled in as I reshuffled self-images, down-shifted and turned around to pick up the skinny kid who was still standing there by the highway with nothing to lose but his blind faith in human kindness.

13

Searching for a Wife

My mother immediately liked Terry the first time she saw her. I could see it in her eyes that day I arrived home with this new woman.

It turned out that my folks were excellent judges of character, but there remains something inexplicable about their approval back then. The oddest part is the fact that Terry was wearing an old army canteen cover for a shoe that had been lost. We had just hitchhiked several hundred miles and we looked like street urchins from mid-nineteenth century Russia. For a first introduction to a new girlfriend, all the cards were stacked against me, but somehow my mother was smiling.

Why was Terry wearing a canteen cover for a shoe, you might ask? Well, it got lost the night before when we were sleeping out on the hillside of the Washington Monument. I think it got lost somewhere between John Denver and James Taylor. Terry and I were there in protest of the Vietnam War. We had participated in a march and now this, an all-night vigil complete with music. There were only about fifty thousand people there and one of them either stole her left sneaker or it just got kicked away in the confusion of people sleeping and waking up on a dewy and overcrowded Potomac hillside. Whatever it was, when morning light arrived, the shoe was gone and the best we could come up with was the canteen cover. The fit was not that bad but we had a lot of walking to do to get out to the Interstate.

Terry and I had found our separate ways to D.C. the day before. She was headed down with a church group of some sort and I was snagging rides from truckers and briefcase salesmen. We had agreed to meet at the foot of the monument at a certain time but when we got there we found that it was a mob scene. I located one person I recognized, a truly obnoxious Marxist from school, but he had not seen Terry. So I wandered and ambled. I went up to at least three young women with torn, multi-patched blue jeans and long brown hair, expecting them to be Terry but they all turned out to be somebody else.

And then I think we just bumped into each other. One of the guys in the church group she had come with had turned creepy, she said, and she was more than glad to see me. I was just feeling slightly bewildered, a little bit lonely and lost like I was always feeling in those days, so I was happy to find her.

We marched a bit, caught some speeches, got seriously angry at the government yet one more time. In the marches, I ran into maybe half a dozen people I had met before from up and down the Eastern Seaboard. Drivers who had picked me up hitchhiking. Even the guy who had picked me up in Atlanta and had driven me all the way home to Jersey with seventy pounds of his radar equipment sitting on my lap. We all felt a sense of family. And then the big sleepover on the hill — Terry and I snuggled into adjoining sleeping bags. I don't know what other generations do without a war to fight against. Some of them just fought in the wars or a lot of them just passed through their turbulent early twenties without the psychic adrenalin of a cause. But not us.

Like other lovers, a war had brought us together. The march had turned from a serious protest into a party. I woke up in the middle of the night when the twentieth person tripped over me and fell to the ground, apologizing. Maybe he had grabbed onto the shoe in a drug-hazy movement; maybe he had walked off with Terry's sneaker and inadvertently sealed my fate. I lay there on my back with this sleeping girl in my arms and I tilted my head far back until that great dark obelisk hovered threateningly above me. I focused on the flashing red light at the tip and then looked up to the few stars that could be seen above. I wondered what it would be like if I had not found her that day and if I was sleeping alone on this noisy, dark hillside. Maybe then I would have felt more like a soldier. Now I just felt like a lover. This is what it was like to grow up and not fight in a war.

Terry and I awoke in a gray dawn. A thin, dreary mist hovered like a marijuana cloud over us all. Bodies were strewn everywhere. It was a vision of upheaval and chaos. Only a few souls walked upright, staggering toward the already over-loaded outhouses. It could have been a scene out of a war. But it wasn't. We rolled up the sleeping bags, shook the dew out of our hair, discovered the missing shoe, lashed the canteen around Terry's foot, and made off for a seventy-nine cent breakfast at Seven Eleven. I'm sure I offered her my workboots to wear on the long journey home but she must have refused.

Almost twenty years later I wake up on another misty morning with the same woman beside me. Wars have come and gone. Dreams have been realized, others have failed or lost importance. I think of the gentlest of protesters who had stayed behind after the demonstration to clean up the grounds of the Washington Monument. We were not among them but I know they were there. The ones who felt responsible to clean up after the rowdies. I like to think that one of them found the shoe, saw some significance to it, and carried it over to the Smithsonian a few short blocks away convincing a curator that this was a symbol of something important. In my gently haunted memory I can still imagine a discussion about the value and meaning of that unmatched shoe.

But if the lost sneaker did not turn up in the gathered morning trash, then certainly someone must have stolen (or as we would have said then, "liberated") the shoe in the night. Someone else who had lost one her own. But then, where did the canteen cover come from? That too was lying on the ground, presumably lost by another protester. Maybe there was an endless chain of lost and found that night that led many of us into husbands and wives. The potential inter-connectedness is staggering.

Whatever the sequence, I know that the end result was the first time my mother had ever seen me with a girl who had a canteen cover on her foot. And in the warmth of my parents' kitchen, the cruelty of a collapsing war seemed diminished by the beginning of another kind of history that supersedes the gravity of military strategy and patriotic plundering.

14

My Vasectomy

I had my vasectomy on a cold day in December halfway through my thirty-sixth year. I had been somewhat slow to arrive at the decision but ultimately it became clear that the time had arrived. The thought, however, of a stranger taking a very sharp instrument to that rather sensitive part of the male anatomy is a frightening notion to any man. Me included. But once all the information was tallied, a vasectomy was, for me, the logical form of birth control.

I knew of perhaps seven other men who had undergone the operation. Some of them told me that the whole business was a bit more painful than what the medical propaganda suggested. One of them had experienced fairly severe complications. Another had gone surfing a few hours after the surgery and, as a result, was obliged to return for a second slice and stitch. All, however, had returned to normal life. Each of them had been in their late thirties and had arrived at the decision in the same reasoned, cautious way I had. There was some personal comfort in thinking that if they could handle it, so could I.

I read what I could in popular medical books and in magazines. I looked for a good single book on the subject but there was none except a 1974 classic which seemed a bit out of date. Then I began to wonder: did I really want to know all the possible complications and everything that could go wrong? Maybe I did, just in case, but I found no easy access in books to the information. So I went to my family doctor, a somewhat curt matter-of-fact, old-school physician named Maloney. I had been in the delivery room for the birth of my daughter with Dr. Maloney. He had reminded me of a quarterback about to receive the ball from the front line. All had gone well despite the fact that it had seemed too much like a sporting event. I wondered what his attitude toward vasectomies would be.

Dr. Maloney didn't try to talk me out of the vasectomy, but he suggested that "if everything is going okay, why fool around with it?" (It was the old philosophy that my father might have offered up: "If it's not broken, don't try to fix it.") My wife wasn't having any complications with the pill now and it was preventing pregnancy, so why worry?

But I had read all those articles at the prompting of my wife. Too many years on birth control pills means trouble. I wanted to live to a ripe old age and I wanted some company. Dr. Maloney was dubious of anything read in the popular press but he could see I was serious. He realized that I was on the road to a vasectomy. He had given me his obligatory cautioning and now he'd get on with the details.

He drew me a little illustration, not unlike ones I had seen on men's rooms walls over North America. The man was not an artist. A tiny squiggly tube led from each testicle to the penis. A section of each tube would be snipped out and the tubes would be tied in neat little knots. I was an expert at knots in Boy Scouts and I wanted to know what kind. Square? Bowline? Bowline on a bight? Sheep shank? He said he didn't know. *What if the guy goofed and tied a slippery old grannie knot?* I wanted to know. *What if he hadn't been trained as well as I had been as a Tenderfoot?* Maloney said he was sorry, he didn't know

124

that much about knots but he was sure it would be a good sturdy one, whatever it was.

I was warned that the odds of reversing the operation were not good. It had been done before, but nobody was handing out guarantees. More importantly, the operation was not *intended* to be reversible. The idea of permanent change worried me. Permanent *anything* worried me. I shelved the worry for later.

There would be a small incision on either side of the scrotum, I was told, and that would be stitched up afterwards. I had my choice: I could opt for a local or a total anaesthetic. My initial reaction was to go for the local, for the "freezing," as the medical profession euphemistically says.

What happens to the prostate? I also wanted to know. I had read somewhere (in the popular press) that there could be complications with the ignoble prostate, that bane to elder malehood. Dr. Maloney said that he knew of no specific worries but that something eventually went wrong with the prostate gland anyway, sooner or later. Small comfort.

An appointment was made for me to visit a urologist, a Dr. Ling, who would do the vasectomy. That would be a month later. To tell you the truth, I decided to put the whole thing out of my mind for a while.

When I went to see Dr. Ling for the first time, he again cautioned me about irreversibility and wanted me to be sure I was ready. I was quite happy to see that the medical profession had not met me with knife-happy greed. Reason and calm prevailed on all fronts. Dr. Ling, who seemed to have cornered the local market in vasectomies, drew me the same crude picture as Maloney had. He told me about haematomas this time; that is, there would probably be a swelling after the operation due to excess blood. But I was not to worry. It would go away of its own accord or with ice packs. "Okay," I gulped. We set an appointment.

"Now," Dr. Ling queried, "would you like a local anaesthetic or general one?" I must have appeared baffled because he asked again, " Would you like freezing of the area or do you want us to put you to sleep?" The question was very matter-of-fact. It was like he was asking me if I wanted my pizza with or without pepperoni.

I didn't like the ring of "being put to sleep." It sounded too much like what one did to an old and failing favored pet. And, in fact, I think that I had already decided I preferred the local. Maybe it was because of some movie I saw with Paul Newman as a lawyer for a client whose husband had died on the operating table during a minor operation. It had been death due, according to the erudite Newman, to improper use of a general anaesthetic. The patient had vomited while unconscious and suffocated to death.

Another image swam up in my head, however, while the polite Dr. Ling smiled passively in my direction, waiting for me to place my order. I considered the power of my imagination. What would it be like to lie there, legs apart, trying to think happy thoughts while a stranger in a white gown took a very sharp knife to my groin? And what would I say to the attending nurses to keep up my end of the conversation? Even if I was frozen into arctic bliss in that lower region, what would my restless imagination conjure up? What fears? What worries? What terror?

"What sort of general anaesthetic is it?" I asked

"Sodium pentothal," the doctor answered.

I liked the sound of it. Sodium pentothal. Wasn't that the truth serum?

"It's very good," he added. The words could have meant almost anything.

"I'll take it," I said flatly, sounding like I had just ordered a new Toyota off the lot.

"How long before I can have sex after that?" I asked. My final worry.

"Ten days to two weeks." He continued to smile his polite, professional smile.

"That long?" Somehow I thought that element of recovery would be brief.

"Needs time to heal," Dr. Ling added with finality.

As I left the office I felt a certain degree of relief and even satisfaction. The decision had been made, belated as it was. I was thankful that it was the late twentieth century and medicine was so advanced. Everything would be smooth and, like the doc, matter-of-fact. I should caution myself against making a big deal of the whole affair.

Driving home, I had to remind myself that, minor as it may be, I was soon to be lying on a hospital outpatient table undergoing surgery, totally unconscious and in the hands of people I did not know, men and women who the profession had licensed as competent. I had not been in a hospital for anything similar since I was eight years old and I had my tonsils removed. Few of my generation seemed to weather those times of tonsil-hating with our tonsils intact. Years later, it was agreed that it had been a bit of a fad, that all too many of us slipped off into the ether while the surgeon snipped. I do recall from my early experience enjoying unconsciousness, however, and it was followed by a lot of ice cream.

I now had to recognize, as well, that in a few more years, vasectomies would improve. They would be reversible, for example. Hadn't I read somewhere about a tiny gold valve that could be installed? Or was that reserved for kings and princes? Or would the vasectomy turn out to be another medical fad? It could be superseded by something much simpler, much cleaner. Or a pill maybe. And then, of course, some researcher was bound to discover yet-undiscovered side effects for those of us who had vasectomies. The bad news would not arrive for years, though.

My self-satisfaction began to fray around the edges. Still, I had done my reading; I had grilled those who had sought the knife before me, and I had spoken to two men of the profession. All things considered, my decision seemed like an intelligent one.

But, of course, it was not really ever my decision. It was arrived at mutually between my wife and myself, slowly over a period of maybe five years. The pill would have to go, and we both had good reason to be leery of all other means of birth control.

Surgery was originally scheduled for 8 a.m. on a Tuesday in November. That would mean getting up at 6 a.m. to be at the hospital by 7. Bad news all around. Dr. Ling had assured me that he was at his peak performance first thing in the morning but obligations in the extreme early morning carried ill-tidings for me. Two weeks later I changed the date of the operation to coincide with my semester break at the university where I teach. He allowed me to reschedule for 10 a.m. on a Wednesday in mid-December. If I turned out to be bed-ridden for a week, I'd have no obligations.

I was requested to go in for a hospital visit a week early for a blood test. No problem. The nurse complimented me on how well my veins protruded in my arms, making her task so much easier. But then I was asked for a urine sample. A new crisis. No one had told me. I had dutifully relieved my bladder before taking the chair for a blood sample. Thankfully, it was a very small sample container that I was given as I was ushered into a washroom. After a few minutes, the will prevailed and I was free to leave the clinic.

Now that I was fully convinced that I was truly on the road to a vasectomy I was ready to get a bit of mileage out of the whole thing. It would rescue me from at least one tedious faculty meeting. I publicly let it be known that I could not attend because it was scheduled for the morning of my vasec-tomy. I noted the diverse reactions from men and women as I began to flaunt my impending hospital visit. Men flinched. Clearly it was an uncomfortable thought. Some reached toward their crotches in involuntary, protective maneuvers. Several women seemed to be offended that I had mentioned such a personal business at all. It was like I had just physically exposed myself by the mere mention of a vasectomy. Yet, other women tended to be quite impressed. ("Another man taking on the responsibility for once.") In my own small way, I was beginning to see that my cheery attitude toward my vasectomy could make me a minor feminist hero. For once in my life I was to be deleted from the rank and file of male chauvinists. I rather liked the feeling. I decided I would discuss my vasectomy freely whenever given the opportunity.

Aside from the occasional public announcement of my immanent act of heroism, I thought very little about it again until the proverbial night before. Up until then, my mind was cluttered with the usual business of day-to-day living. But, because of the general anaesthetic to be administered, I was given strict orders "not to take water, food, drink or anything by the mouth after midnight." I could eat supper, but I decided against a snack or anything that evening. Err on the safe side, I figured.

I had also been instructed that I was to shave before I arrived at the hospital. It wasn't just a matter of looking respectable. I had been asked to shave the hairs off of a section of my personal geography that had never before been groomed in such a way. Thus, I found myself sitting down with my trusty Remington electric attempting the impossible. After the demented little machine yanked several obstinate hairs out by the root, I declared that I was using the wrong tool. Electric razors were no good for the business at hand.

I retreated to the bathroom and located one fairly new disposable razor. But no shaving cream. Warm water and soap suds would have to do. And in order to find the correct position for this feat, I was required to undertake several ballet-like stances with one foot positioned high up at the sink. Even then I was baffled as to exactly where I was to shave. I admitted to myself that I didn't know precisely where the incisions would be made but it was too late to call up the good doctor for shaving advice. I did the best I could and succeeded in finishing without shedding a drop of blood.

Afterwards, I went to bed and I had a lousy night's sleep. Obligatory. I could drink nothing in the morning, not even water. I didn't eat breakfast for maybe the third time in my entire existence. No problem. In fact, I decided, I was actually fasting. I had gone fourteen hours without food or drink. This was probably as pure as I was ever going to get. I felt downright spiritual.

And so, as the sun brightens up the land, the traffic and the shopping malls of Christmas, the day has finally arrived. Soon, I'm walking through the front doors of a modern community hospital. I take a number, like in a deli or a pastry shop . . . and wait. When my number is called I sit down with a woman and a computer terminal. She asks a few basic questions about address and wife. Then, she asks, "What religion are you? You don't have to answer if you don't want to." I want to ask her why she wants to know but others are waiting; it's not a time for religious debate. I give a generic answer, "Christian," just to keep things moving. There are a lot of people with higher numbers than me.

Questions about religion always make me think of death. The hospital wants to know which cleric to call in if I bite the big one in the out-patient surgery. Or maybe it's more than that. Perhaps the hospital computer is patched straight into the hereafter. If you die on the operating table, the hospital can direct your soul to the appropriate form of heaven or nirvana or whatever. A slip on the keys by the admitting personnel could send an unlucky Methodist to a realm where he is surrounded by Hindus. These are some of the last minute worries of one about to be vasectomized.

With the quiz over, I'm directed to a place called the "Day Surgery," which sounds to me a lot like a day nursery, a place where children go to play. I hand the attending nurse in the day surgery my file and take a seat by a very nervous man who doesn't want to remove his winter coat. "How is it going?" I ask.

"Not good. I don't like this place."

I look around. Things actually seem quite cheery, clean and bright. Brisk doctors are making jokes. Patients at the other end of the room are being called back from unconsciousness in polite, insistent tones. All seems in order.

My companion tells me he's in for some work on his nose. He doesn't get specific. "What about you?" he asks.

"I'm here for my vasectomy," I say. It's funny how I've personalized it. I'm reminded of those old articles in *Reader's Digest*: "I Was Lesley's Vasectomy."

"Oh, you're here to be sterilized," the nose man chimes in.

Yee, Gads. It's true. I hadn't really thought of it that way. I mean, I hadn't used that term on myself. Neither had anyone else. I was here to voluntarily become sterile. The word had ominous overtones. "Well, yes, I guess so," I admit. The worrier shakes his head. "I just hope you wake up."

I laugh nervously, the word *sterilization* caught like a fish hook in my consciousness.

"Mr. Choyce?" the nurse asks, rescuing me from doubt.

I wave. She hands me a pile of hospital garb and points to a changing room.

I reappear with green paper slippers, a johnny shirt, and a green shower cap of sorts. I'm directed to a gurney and asked to lie down. A new nurse comes to take by blood pressure and asks me several questions that I can't answer because of the thermometer shoved in my mouth. Around me pre-op patients chat nervously.

I've held onto a book to occupy my mind and as I lie waiting for nearly an hour, I read about a small town in Minnesota during the nineteenth century.

Dr. Ling arrives looking relaxed and dapper. He checks to see how my shaving work went. It isn't until later that I discover I shaved in completely the wrong place. Dr. Ling doesn't let on his dissatisfaction with my handiwork. A few minutes later, I'm wheeled down a hallway into a small unassuming operating room. I practice being helpless and lie back on my rolling table as it bumps along.

Once in the O.R., I'm introduced to my anaesthetist, an attractive well-tanned woman who looks too young for the job. She competently jabs a needle into my arm and hooks me up to a dripping bottle of something. It all looks very convincing. The anaesthetist is joined by another youngish lady in white and the doctor. I wonder if I should feel self-conscious about exposing my semi-shaved privates to the women but decide it would serve no purpose.

I watch the bottle drip into me and wait for unconsciousness, thankful I won't have to hang around for idle chit-chat during the operation. A new fear comes over me as I watch the preparations: *I'm wide awake.* "How soon does the drug take effect?" I ask the anaesthetist.

"Oh, it only takes seconds," she tells me.

"That's funny," I say, "I don't feel anything."

"That's because we haven't given you anything yet."

"Oh."

I try relaxing and look up at the indifferent ceiling.

"Well, here ya go," she says after a bit. It's the same thing my mother said on my first trip to the dentist. I watch as she inserts something else into the tube that is attached to my arm. "The next thing you know, you'll be in recovery." Easy for her to say.

But she is right. The fade into unconsciousness is all too brief. It seems like fun but the lights go out quickly. In recovery, like all the others, I would prefer to keep on snoring but there are more to follow in day surgery and the bed is needed. Recognizing that a sodium pentothal sleep is a very deep one, I had been hoping for some minor revelation, prompting myself for it, even. In fact, it seems that something is revealed to me from burrowing around that low in my subconscious. Or maybe it is just one of my many private delusions. Whatever it is, I try to hold onto the thought, the image or whatever it is, to the very brink of consciousness. But as soon as I open my eyes, it's gone. I am awake, back in the world of the living. The operation is over. The sleep is over. I'm a renovated man. The nurse is reminding me of where I am. I feel like sleeping more and am disappointed that I'll have to get up and mosey on shortly. As soon as she sees that she has done her mission of tugging me back into the wide-awake world, she moves on to another sleeper.

Time for a quick systems check. Not much pain. A little soreness in the obvious region but less than expected. It reminds me vaguely of the time I was eleven years old. The chain came off my bicycle and my crotch came down hard on that bar put on boys' bikes exclusively for masochistic purposes. It feels like that a little bit, but not so bad.

No headache, no nausea. No real, honest-to-goodness hurt to speak of. I decide against touching with my hands, certain there's some blood or stitching that I'll discover soon enough.

I'm offered coffee or juice. I opt for caffeine. Within an hour, I'm back changing into my street clothes and I walk to my wife in a nearby waiting room. She's been Christmas shopping while I was unconscious but has returned in time to find me slightly wobbly, a tiny bit giddy, but more or less willing to leave the comforts of sodium pentothal and hospital life for the trip home.

I walk a little weird . . . like I just arrived home to Abilene after a thirty-day cattle drive. The stitches feel stiff and annoying and cause me to parade bow-legged through the lobby. I'm using muscles that don't usually get a workout. I'm sure other men have returned to work the same day. I don't have to so I lounge in bed at home, or sit around reading more about life in that small nineteenth-century Minnesota town until I grow restless.

I had been expecting to lay low for a few days to enjoy a bit of consolation and sympathy as a side-effect of the operation. But it turns out that I prefer the opposite. I find myself doing house work and attending to some business details. Three days later, the waves are good and I want to go surfing. My wife gets militant and insists that it's too soon for strenuous activity. She reminds me of my friend who went surfing too soon and tore out his stitches.

I try to relax, but on the fourth day, I find myself returning to the university for yet another department meeting. When things get sluggish, I complain that my wounds are bothering me and would they mind moving things along a bit quicker. It's only half-true, really, but I'm successful in trimming a full hour off the event, thanks to my colleagues' compassion.

The following day, I put on my winter surfing gear and go to the ocean. I surf cautiously but return home feeling confident that I am fully recovered.

As the dissolvable stitches work their way out of the flesh, they feel hard, sharp, and very uncomfortable. I end up trimming them down. One morning there is a bit of blood engorging in the scrotum, the predicted haematoma. It's uncomfortable but not painful. I make a visit to Dr. Maloney who tells me it's normal and that I should put an ice pack on it. The swelling goes down and, aside from taking long hot baths every day, my life is nearly one hundred percent back to normal.

After another three or four months, Terry will be able to stop taking the birth control pill if my follow-up tests prove that the vasectomy was a success. Apparently, the wily human body is often capable of reattaching the vas deferens even after the cutting and the knot-tying. It seems we're a species quite adept at perpetuating itself against all odds.

Once I am 100% certain that I am back to normal, I experience a second minor phase of self-congratulatory heroism. I'm proud of how well I've handled the *Big V.* and would like to go public. Maybe I should write an entire book about vasectomies and then go on an international promotion tour. "Let's let all the women off the pill who don't want to get pregnant," I'll say on *Donahue*. Or I might quip, "Heck, I downright enjoyed my vasectomy. I'd have another one if they'd let me." Or something to that effect. Maybe I'd carry around photographs of my scars. Or better yet, maybe TV would come up with some tasteful way that I could show off Dr. Ling's handiwork. I can hear Oprah now saying, "Lance, could we pull in for a tight shot? There, that's good." The camera would linger perhaps for a few seconds, I'd take a deep breath and there would be applause fading into a commercial break for pie crust or salad dressing.

Instead, I make a phone call to a local radio producer to see if they would like to talk about my vasectomy on the CBC. "I just had one," I said. "It was great."

"Hmm," she said. "No, we did vasectomies about five years ago. It was a hot topic then. Vasectomies just don't have the public profile they once did. They are over the hill as far as we are concerned at Current Affairs."

"Oh," I said, my male ego once again demolished. I was not at the cutting edge of anything after all.

"But if you had like a really bizarre side effect, we'd definitely be interested. Or if you came up with a really unique disease or infection of any sort, we'd be glad to have you on."

"Sorry," I said. "It's just a little sore is all."

"That's not good enough," the producer said. "Better luck next time."

15

Waiting Out Dinner

I am waiting. Simply waiting for the wind to change directions. When you live along the coast, the direction of the wind is very important. Onshore, offshore. North or south. Clear bright blue or blustery blue grey. If the wind goes east, everything goes rotten. If it slaps from the west, it can evoke passion or paranoia. But here on the coast there is an exaggerated longing for anything to change. Right now the wind is nearly dead. Just a light, indifferent sea breeze. There's nothing outside but a woolly womb of gray. I am waiting for the wind to change.

Waiting is a powerful game. Full of love and hate and awkward stony moments. An interruption between what was and what will be. There is a broken promise. You fall into a crack, an abyss of possibility, of becoming, but not accepting.

I don't usually feel like this. But the waiting today is over-powering. That's why my imagination is in handcuffs, why I sit back in the spindled wooden rocker and look at my hands. This is what it will be like to be old if I am not careful.

One day I will wake up and find I am waiting to die. Days will seem short but they will all run together. Sooner or later I'll forget who I am. Or I'll think I'm still a boy waiting to go sledding or ice skating. Worse yet, lying awake in bed in an early morning, waiting for my mother to call me down to breakfast which will be followed by school.

I did some of my worst waiting in school. Long math classes. Someone had lashed down the minute hand with invisible chains. Time, frozen like a decimal point, the world arrested, stopped from spinning.

Or waiting for the courage to act upon an impulse. To tell someone I was in love with her. Endless interior revisions until the moment was too late.

My mind usually acts on my behalf. It doesn't like to wait. It busies itself with the rubric of living. Often it finds important things for me to do. Together, my mind and I are opposed to the whole murder of time. We do useful things together, eventually co-opting the body to participate until we have accomplished some damn thing or another and are very pleased with all of us. By then it's dinner time and we have annihilated waiting and time altogether.

Early February and waiting for disappointment. The ice will not melt. Spring will not arrive soon enough. We will see the sun by July if we can wait it out. Snow at least is a cutting loose. Fog can be an avalanche of nothingness if you have the wrong attitude.

Sometimes, lying awake in the middle of the night, I am waiting for a very powerful dream of some sort to let me know who I am. I lay awake, receptive, waiting. Something somewhere is holding back.

Time can be ambushed with physical activity until it dissolves. The mind is often alert and happy to let the body work on its own once in a while. It gets involved as best it can and congratulates the body on what it can do. But too much mental activity gets on the nerves of anyone's physical carcass. Sometimes it's worth running out onto the foggy ice and shouting just to see if anything happens. Will I fall through the ice? Will the geese stir from the open waters and rush south?

Will I be shot dead by a waiting hunter? Or will the dream blossom from inside?

Things to do while waiting: sorting, stapling papers, writing cheques, drinking coffee, listening to phone-in talk shows with visiting veterinarians, reading a book about North American Indians, unpacking boxes, packing boxes, making annoying phone calls, trying to memorize jokes. Sit down and write something about the only thing in your head.

Waiting it out. Staring down eternity. Outside, I can see the snow has melted from my overturned green canoe. The canoe looks like it is dreaming fibreglass dreams of summer.

The sky is getting darker and the wind has not changed. My own impact on the world has diminished to microscopic dust as I sit and grieve for lost time, lost chances. Nothing much can happen now.

Tomorrow the wind will howl from the north. The day will be angry and full of change. The waiting will be over. Someone will have returned. Something will have spliced my life back together. But for now, all I have to look forward to is dinner, that commonest of family rituals.

I must be getting old. This is truly the first that I've noticed it but the evidence is clear. It's two o'clock in the afternoon and I'm thinking about dinner. Up to this point in my life I have been so pre-occupied with everything I do that I don't think much about food until it is on a fork headed for my mouth. But it's two o'clock in the afternoon and I'm thinking that dinner is something to look forward to.

I'll admit it's a so-so day. A few interesting details happened. I did a longish radio interview from my home phone with a Toronto radio host concerning the new burrowing nuclear weaponry that Frank Carlucci at the Pentagon has proposed. He's ticked off about the Soviet military underground bunkers. Now he'll have weapons to root them out like truffle-sniffing pigs.

I also found out the new line-up of guests for my TV show including no less than Ample Annie, a long-time stripper and porno film star who has written a book about how the criminal types have taken over the striptease business. But, so far, this has all been phone work and not part of the real world. The expected miracles of the day have not arrived yet and by mid-afternoon it looks hopeless. I'll settle into class preparations and an afternoon of, if I get motivated, invoicing. Invoicing brings out the worst in me and I feel a tight constriction around my heart. No, I won't invoice.

Instead, I try reading a little something by Joan Didion but I get distracted because suddenly I am looking forward to dinner. Dinner tonight will not be anything special. My wife will cook something. She is a good cook and superhumanly capable of making a meal of basic (let's call it honest) good food in a matter of fifteen minutes. She doesn't rely on prepared foods. It's just that she doesn't mess around. If it were late summer, I could walk to the garden, dawdle around the pumpkins to check for girth, eat a few remaining raw peas from the withered branches, harvest some parsley, lettuce, beet greens, a small zucchini, and some Swiss chard.

Then I would make the salad. It takes me longer to make a salad than it does for my wife to cook up and serve all the food. It's an enigma to me but salads I make slowly. It's a comforting ritual after discussing nuclear death or thinking about TV interviews with Ample Annie. Other people chant, look for inner lights or concentrate on their breathing. I make very slow salads. But, sadly, it is winter and I can't partake of salad therapy.

So, eventually my daughter, my wife, and I will sit down to dinner. There is nothing at all extraordinary about it. I will have to get up four to seven times to locate and retrieve items not on the table and absolutely essential to the complete meal. Things like a sharp knife, a bottle of Worcestershire sauce, some pickled beets, vinegar, or maybe we have just run out of salt.

Usually the dog is begging at the table for food and almost always my daughter (nine now) says she'd rather be in the living room, eating in front of a cartoon show called *Duck Tales.*

Inevitably the phone rings. Toronto and Winnipeg are still in the last throes of a business day and I have news (good or bad) from a printer or an editor. Long distance calls, at least, are quick; small talk is minimal.

The meal is exceedingly ordinary except for the fact that all of the food tastes good. Basic stuff: potatoes, broccoli, maybe a bit of ham or pork or chicken. Food. Dinner.

We usually argue a bit over dinner. My daughter starts most of the arguments these days. Once I was the argument starter with minor household complaints. Then it was my wife. Now we have both given up arguments because my daughter likes to start them so often. They are always trivial and based on indefensible remembrances of what one of us said or did not say. Sometimes there is the threat of carrying around portable tape recorders so it is perfectly clear what the parent said or did not say. The arguments don't go anywhere at all but they don't escalate into warfare, either. Sometimes there is a radio on in the background with news that three-fourths of Bangladesh is under water and the country is being overrun by poisonous snakes and dysentery.

I should point out that we always eat at five o'clock if at all possible. Five o'clock is the time people should eat dinner. It's the sign of a truly civilized culture. Anything later indicates to me a civilization in decay. Anything earlier means you're headed to the fat farm. Five o'clock is just about right. It gets the work day over with quickly and gives you a long evening to goof around as a family.

Since so little happens around here at dinner — aside from minor disagreements, phone calls, dog problems, food shuttles, and eating, why am I looking forward to dinner at two in the afternoon? I think it's because I'm getting old. I've worked in nursing homes. There, life revolves around meals. Meals are everything. I'm too young for nursing homes and have much to live for other than food but still it's a nondescript afternoon and I'm looking forward to dinner. I think this means I have finally grown up. I am, alas, an adult now. I like the idea of my small family sitting down in a warm kitchen sharing an evening meal.

The corniness of this small portrait is nearly beyond my comprehension, but there you have it. I guess I just like the way that the world whittles itself down to that small space around the wobbly formica-topped kitchen table where we all sit. Maybe when I am finally and truly old and senile, that's what I'll remember about my life in my mid-thirties. Maybe the rest will be erased from the program, accidentally deleted from the disk. If so, I won't be completely morose. I'll have the memory of dinner perhaps, and this quiet, unimportant afternoon to remember. I'll remember looking forward to dinner and that just might be enough.

16
Publishing Without Clothes

Maybe it's because we've had a very warm season in Nova Scotia. Or maybe it's because publishers are sometimes called self-indulgent and I'm beginning to believe it. Whatever the reason, I've begun publishing naked.

Yes, without clothes on. Publishing in the nude as they would have said in the early 1960s.

Since "publishing" seems like such a public affair, my actions could perhaps be considered by some to be unconscionable or even criminal. In truth, I haven't yet gone out onto the streets to do my publishing work without some form of sartorial assistance. What would the booksellers make of it? The managers at the Coles and W.H. Smith stores change so often that none would recognize me as I appeared on my appointed rounds. They would phone immediately for mall security before I had a chance to show them this year's new volumes of poetry or fiction. Of the more conservative booksellers, I could expect to lose a few accounts. No, I don't think it would make much sense.

Instead, most of my naked publishing happens in the privacy of my second storey office in my old farmhouse at

Lawrencetown Beach. That's where I operate Pottersfield Press. The tourists are arriving and I see them sunning themselves on the beach. Why shouldn't I too be shedding some clothes even if I am indoors publishing away to my heart's content?

When the Purolator man comes to the back door with a dispatch from my printer, he says that he's surprised . . . shocked and appalled, that I greet him in the all-together. He says he didn't know we went in for that kind of publishing on the Eastern Shore. So now I'm gaining a bad reputation with the courier services.

Perhaps I should pause here for a moment to explain what a publisher does, or at least what this publisher does in the buff.

I edit manuscripts, for one thing. I trim off unnecessary phrases and whole paragraphs, pare down prose, toss off excess verbiage like old, useless clothing. I have no problem doing this in the nude.

I argue with the typesetter and printer over the phone quite comfortably without a stitch on. (The office is warm; a sultry breeze caresses my ribcage.) Then there's the business of doing book layout. Herein lies danger. Exacto knives often take on a life of their own, fall off drawing tables and threaten laceration or even castration. Deadly and unpredictable spray glues are sometimes used and a gust of wind can send the sticky stuff almost anywhere.

Invoicing without clothes on is no problem, however. Numbers are almost never offended by nakedness and calculators have not a Puritan streak among them.

Packaging presents a small problem; again with knives and tape dispensers (or guns as they are sometimes called). All of this can be handled with practice.

I write quite a few letters at my word processor. Instead of a proper computer monitor I still use an old twelve inch black and white TV set. I have yet to discover if there is any potential damage to a TV set from long-term exposure to nudity. No doubt a study is already underway on this subject in the psychology department of a small midwestern American college. As for the effect on me when I write . . . letters or my own prose and poetry . . . I feel freer, less constrained. I don't sweat as much.

Certainly other publishers have worked through torrid seasons before. Why is it I've never heard of other publishers working in stark nakedness? What is it that makes them keep their pants zipped and their shirts buttoned throughout this often thankless, sometimes humiliating, often knotty task? Is it grim determination? A sense of moral responsibility? Are they high Anglicans or simply too modest? I'm not sure. For some of us, though, publishing is like making love. Neither task should be performed with clothes on.

I'm not sure. Maybe others are doing it already and I don't know about it. There are ten fairly well established publishers in Nova Scotia. I phoned them all this afternoon and discovered that I was the only one publishing without my clothes on. That's one out of ten. Perhaps this is the norm across the country.

What will happen once the news is out? Surely, someone from the CBC will want to interview one of us. Cameras will be brought in to our publishing houses. There will be an uproar for I am on the receiving end of certain government subsidies. The Minister of Communications will have to answer the question from some gravely-voiced opposition member: "Will the Honourable Minister explain to the good people of Canada why their tax money is going to men and women who publish in such an indecent manner?" An uproar will follow, a public inquiry. When it has been discovered that such and such a book on the shelves was created by a publisher while he had his clothes off, it will be wrenched from the racks. Regardless of content. But I hope it never comes to that.

Those who write about the book trade will try to uncover the truth behind this new phenomenon. They will try to explain that it has something to do with Free Trade or the GST or Censorship laws or government support for culture; or maybe it is some sort of statement about society itself. (Always, the search goes on for the naked truth.) We will be called literary nudists or underclothed bibliophiles or even unclad bibliomaniacs who flaunt conventions. Several Ph.D. students in the English Department at York University will defend Ph.D. dissertations in the year 2010 concerning, "Naked Canadian Publishing in the Late Twentieth Century."

But maybe I'm wrong. Perhaps I am the only one publishing without clothes on in all of Canada. I'm sure, however, that there are other *writers* working without a stitch on. I've met several poets on the Pacific shoreline at Wreck Beach. Free spirits of free verse who knew that the body was just another book that needed to be laid bare, given sunlight and exposure if it wanted an audience.

But alas, winter will soon be here. I'll stoke the woodstove till it glows but it won't be enough. I'll put my clothes on. I'll go back to being a regular publisher. It's not what I want, believe me. I'll leave the privacy of Pottersfield Press and venture out into the world to gossip with writers and consult with government officials and even consort with the public who may want to buy some of my books. I'll be wearing pants, a shirt, and even a tie just for pure sarcasm. Underneath the fashionable exterior, however, will still beat the heart of a naked publisher, someone who knows that the best publishing work in this country is done without clothes on, all alone, without the cumbersome voyeurism of a curious and sometimes critical public.

17

Dumping Ground

I was in Toronto for one day. In the afternoon I would read from my new book at the outpatient clinic of the Psychiatric Unit of the Toronto General Hospital. I was very proud of the gig.

But the real story is the woman at the airport. Somebody's mother. Fifty-five maybe. I don't know if she just got off a plane or what but she was waiting for the bus just like me. She wore clip-on sunglasses and when she walked out of the building her radar detected me, a Nova Scotian with two sympathetic ears. She zeroed in, flipped up the sun glasses, and told her story immediately without preface or introduction.

"You think that son of a bitch wants to let us on the bus? Hell no. He gets paid to drink coffee. That's all he does. And he probably doesn't even do that well. This place is nothing but a dumping ground."

I smiled.

"What are you going to do?" she said. "That's the way the world is today. Like my son I was telling you about. I'm here to bring him some food. It's a jungle, he says. And I know 'cause I've seen it too. You can't trust anyone. Now my son, he comes down here to get an education and look what happens

147

to him. Nothing but trouble. He blames it on the seagull . . ."

"Seagull?"

"Yeah, the seagull that stole his food. He had a pizza. I'd given him enough money for a pizza at least but he says he put the pizza down on the bench and a seagull came and took it. I didn't get it at first. What do you mean a seagull took it, I asked him. Seagal, he told me. It's the name of the president of the university.

"Apparently this guy, Seagal, threw my son out of classes. And the bastard wouldn't give him his money back. The creep. So theres's my boy in the middle of July all alone in the city without any money. I come down to see him then and I go to his apartment. He's sitting there in a leather jacket, zipped to the neck. Christ, I tell him . . . I'm there sweating with drips of it going down out of my armpits. Christ, I say, what are you doing with that heavy jacket on?

"Mom, he says, it's all I got left. They stole everything else. Who? I ask. The seagull, he tells me. What can I do? I laugh. He's my boy, you know what I mean. And he's had his problems. He tells me that they steal everything in Toronto if it ain't nailed down to something . . . I believe him. I look around his apartment and there ain't nothing there. That's why my boy's got his jacket on so's they don't steal that. I open up a can of mandarin oranges and offer him one but he says he ain't hungry.

"Oh boy, I should have never let him come into the city. The police is the worst. They'll steal ya blind. But anyway, I go in to this president of the university 'cause it was my money my boy lost on that stupid place which ain't nothing but a dumping ground, I assure you. And I go in to see Mr. Seagull and there he is, eating the god damn pizza. He's got his feet up on his desk. The man is maybe seventy pounds overweight and I can see what he's been doing to my boy. I try to be polite but what can a mother do? He tells me my son was lazy and that's why he was kicked out.

"Fine, I say, just give me my god damn money back. But Seagal, he looks up at me like I just pulled in from maybe somewhere nobody ain't ever heard of and he tells me I can't have my money back. Him sitting there eating my son's pizza.

"Well, if I'd a known what I was up against, I would have planned better, but meanwhile, I figure I better go get some food in my son before he starves. So I get there but he's not around. Later I find that he spent all the money I brought down to him taking a taxi looking for a new apartment. Him in that black leather jacket. I can't imagine what the heat is like inside that thing in July."

It's December now and I'm afraid to ask for an update but I know she's here to see her son.

"I don't know if I'll find him or not now but I got food here. I come all the way down to make sure my boy eats good. I got mandarin oranges, Vienna sausages. Canned things, ya know."

I nod. The bus has arrived. Do I want out of this conversation? I do, but somehow I feel that I need to pay my dues. I need to know the truth, the whole truth.

"Where you from?" she asks.

"Nova Scotia."

"I remember when there used to be places like Nova Scotia," she says with perfect clarity. "Take my advice. This city ain't nothing but a dumping ground."

Her bus pulls up.

"Take good care of yourself," I say. "And say hi to your boy for me."

She flips her sunglasses down over her glasses. The bus driver offers to help her with her shopping bags, but she shows him the point of her elbow as she's swallowed by the bus. I'm left alone on a cold, empty dark bus platform waiting for the connection to York Mills and the subway downtown.

Despite the omen, the day turns out to be full of intel-

ligent, polite people who treat me well: editors, radio inter-
viewers, even the catatonics and the manic depressives at the
hospital. I bring them all news of Nova Scotia and well-being.
They think it's wonderful. I discover that I've spent a lot of
time trying to convince people that we don't have any problems down there at all. It's not a dumping ground like some
other places in the world, I hear myself saying. I find that I
really like these people a whole lot. I exaggerate a bit in my
stories because I really do want them to believe there are
places out there like Nova Scotia, even here, eight stories up
in the middle of a building that takes up a full city block, but
what I'm reading in their faces is something I've heard before
today: "I remember when there used to be places like Nova
Scotia." And as I talk I find myself shifting tense without any
clear reason.

Leaving the hospital I find myself taking the stairs, avoiding
the elevator and the crush of white coats therein. Back on the
street, I discover I've become an anachronism and I fill up with
a sad, sweet nostalgia for home and a past that I've worked hard
to hold onto even as I'm swept along into the indifference of
the future.

18

One Man's Anger

Anger. Male anger. I had almost forgotten about it until last Sunday when it welled up inside me and I, with a short fiery speech, provoked it in another man.

I was driving past the upper lobe of the headland when I saw the truck gouging its way across the field from the sea cliff. I fancy myself as the self-appointed protector of all things natural within several square miles of my home. So, naturally, my blood began to boil. I jerked my car off the road, directly in his path and stopped.

A man roughly my own age, but with the neck of a small rhino, rolled down the window allowing my tirade. I tried to avoid using big words. Words of several syllables dampened the effect of any do-gooders speech thrown together in haste. But I would not stoop to foul language either. Besides, a pretty woman sat beside him on the seat of the cab.

"Don't you realize the damage you're doing to the environment?" I said, sounding a lot like someone's intellectual grandmother.

His eyes immediately glazed over and his nearly new 4 X 4 Nissan truck seemed to aggressively dig in its rubber-toothed wheels and sink deeper into the vulnerable, virgin headland grasses. I had used the worst of all possible words to a maniac with a big truck and a desire to slash gullies from one end of the province to the other. ENVIRONMENT.

My blood still boiled but I knew anything else I could say would be futile. He saw me for what I was. A goddamn environmentalist. Despite recognition of my failure, I pushed on. I tried tact.

"Look, I'm sure if you have a truck like this (I tapped it aggressively with a knuckle), you must appreciate the countryside." I was attempting a sort of perverse backfield logic now. "I'm sure you don't intend to go around wrecking nature." NATURE. Damn, it was the only word I could think of. All hope was gone. The world would be carved and fractured by thousands of Nissan truck wheels. Buddy here would want nothing but revenge. I looked over at the blonde, checking for some response from her. She avoided my eyes. It's true, I appeared to be lunatic. I had just got out of the ocean and peeled down the rubber skin of my dry suit halfway. Two loose and empty arms of rubber flapped at my sides and, as I spoke, it was as if I was some wounded four-armed creature from another planet.

My adversary had not spoken a word. I kept my eyes locked on his. I saw pressure building up in him. I had, alas, made his blood boil as well. Our horns were locked. Worse yet, his girlfriend had listened to me chastise him like a little boy. Then it occurred to me. I had been pushing him. The little speech. *Environment. Nature.* I had tapped a knuckle on his truck. I might as well have kicked his father in the groin right before his face.

It began to sink in that he was ready to get out of his truck and smash me in the face. But I stood my ground. The environment above all else. If I couldn't protect my headland, by Jesus, I'd die in defence of its honor. I kept pushing. "C'mon man, use your senses." I guess I was referring to eyesight because I pointed back to the wet, shiny mud tire canals on the hill. "Look at what you did." I sounded exactly like someone talking to a dog that had just crapped on the living room carpet.

"You think I was the only one who drove up here?" he asked, venom in his voice. But it was a sign of weakness. He had accepted his guilt but was pleading he was no different from other invisible trucks that had come in the night and left their scars. Innocence by group action.

"Well, just think next time before you do this. Please." I wasn't chickening. I was just trying to give him an exit. I had wrecked his day. He had wrecked mine. For whatever reasons, he had decided that I seemed to wield authority, so he didn't smash my face. Maybe it was the extra arms of the flapping drysuit. Maybe the girlfriend. Maybe he knew I was simply right. But there would be no "Golly, gee whiz, I'm sorry." Instead, he sucked me into the final scene.

"You know what?" he snarled, eyes gone red with pent-up rage and frustration, neck bulging beyond human proportions.

"What?"

"I think you're full of shit." He spit the words out.

I was immediately back on the playground. I had played this scene out a million times before. There was no holding back the words.

"No, man. You are," I said.

He shifted into extra-low and spit sods and mud as he drove off, nearly running over my foot and spraying mud as he swerved around my car in his path.

So that was what it ultimately came down to. Two men who were full of shit. I had made another enemy upon the face of the earth. I could have made my point more effectively in a gentle way but I had allowed my masculinity to transform me into a raging (albeit slightly emaciated) bull against a snarling Nissan rhinoceros.

Maybe Helen Caldicott is right. Unless the men let the women take over, civilization is doomed. Only that week I had interviewed Helen on my TV show. I had remained relatively unmoved during the entire show as we had meltdowns aboard American trident subs in Halifax Harbour and rendered much of Nova Scotia uninhabitable for over 10,000 years. We had gone on to destroying life on earth several times over and progressed right into the irrepressible logic of a nuclear winter.

"I've watched the generals," she told my viewing audience. "And you know what? When they're talking about all their missiles, they're just like little boys comparing the size of their penis." In truth, I had never in my entire boyhood taken part in or watched anyone else actually measure their size. I think that old story is just a myth. But I understood the point Helen was getting at.

I was stunned and reeling from the facts: 63,000 nuclear weapons. Canada, allowing nuclear-wielding subs into her harbors, subs that are banned from port in Boston and New York. Military buyers attending military hardware shows in Paris where girls in bikinis stretch across heat-seeking missiles. The reduced strike time — six minutes or less — leading to a launch-on-warning nuclear attack scenario with no hope of recall. We had staged World War Three on TV yet another time and we had survived. My camera man was giving me the wrap up signal.

Yet again, words tripped me up and threw me in the ditch. "So you're hoping that the power will be delivered into the hands of the women in the next few years to straighten out the mess?"

Helen grew livid. I had used the wrong verb.

"Not delivered," she corrected. "We are going to take it and there's going to be a full-scale revolution. It's the only way we can save the planet."

I saw my mistake, began to wimp-out against my formidable guest. Hey, I was on her side, after all. I wasn't the enemy. Or was I? "But certainly men can help out, can't we?"

She saw the look on my face. We had nearly run out of time but the cameras rolled on. "Look, I'm sorry about your precious little male ego but it's just the way it's going to have to be. Sure you can *try* to help. But just don't get in the way."

My mother had just spoken to me from deep inside my childhood kitchen. She was in a panicked frenzy over getting some meal ready and her words had just savaged my ego as I had demanded her attention to some monumental, insignificant detail of my life.

I thanked Helen for her time, closed the show, sat slightly shaken. She had bruised my ego. And it surprised the hell out of me.

Dr. Caldicott gave me a bright, elfin smile, gathered her goods, and nearly sprinted out of my studio on to the next interview a block away. She had five minutes to be on the set at ATV.

It wasn't until a few days later, after my showdown with the Nissanmaster, that I thought again of the male monster in me and worried that maybe Helen was right. Maybe I was never involved in comparative penis sizing but I am a wager of wars. But, of course, so is she. Anyone in favor of disarmament is waging a war against weapons.

Yet, I'm stuck with my anger and self-righteousness. My male anger. Men try to protect through aggression. We always have. Just maybe women could do it differently. If so, I like to think that I'm ready to hand over the reins of power now. No questions asked.

19

Sublime Self-Improvement

A few days ago I received an unsolicited sample of an audio cassette in the mail. It was from a company in Michigan named Potentials Unlimited. I didn't pay attention to the tape right away but got hooked on the promotional material. Barry Konicov, Chairman of the Board over at Potentials, wanted to help me improve my life. Barry looked like a warm, pudgy shrink with a lot of face hair and not much on top who told me, "Only you can make the decision to change, modify, or improve your life."

I thought about it. The decision was mine. Did I, in fact, want to change, modify, or improve my life? I decided that I wasn't sure. Maybe I did, maybe I didn't. A lot depended on how much work it would be and how much the changes, modifications, or improvements would cost. I was reminded of a semi-annual catalogue I used to get from a goliath auto-accessories company in Chicago called J.C. Whitney. They sold thousands of things that would change, modify, or improve your car. Things like Claxton horns, fender skirts, hood ornaments of storks, a trillion things you could plug into your cigarette lighter, fur lining for your dash, and tiny ten-dollar devices that

157

were guaranteed to improve your gas mileage by three hundred percent or your money back. Back in those days the only thing I ever ended up buying was a small cardboard car freshener that smelled of toilet disinfectant but had a colorful picture of a semi-naked woman on it.

But Barry's slogan was this: "One individual communicating truth with conviction is a majority." I liked that. This was such a lofty, quixotic, and all-round illogical statement of principle that I decided I really liked this guy. I read on. His booklet even had page numbers and it went up to page 32. I had published monographs with fewer pages so this was impressive. I read on. Apparently, there were two sides to the tape. One side was for self hypnosis. But large dark typeface ordered: "Warning: Do not play the self-hypnosis side of this tape while driving an automobile."

Already mysterious things were happening in my mind. I was spinning back in time to my days as a Cub Scout. It was my first encounter with a hypnotist. He had arrived as the main attraction at the father-and-son Cub Scout banquet. The hypnotist had coerced three Cub Scouts — Leonard Pozniak, Russell Haines, and Billy Burkin — into being hypnotized in front of the whole gang. He told them that they were no longer Cub Scouts; they were chickens. Sure enough, the air erupted with clucking and scratching. Then he told them they were no longer chickens but they now saw UFOS orbiting around the church hall. Pretty soon it was all over and they were back to normal, which is to say only slightly less strange than when they were hypnotized.

I vowed never to let such a powerful man of mental powers screw around with my mind. But he had also noted that people had been able to "achieve magnificent heights of attainment" through something called *self*-hypnosis. Now there was something for yours truly.

I went back home and searched through my Classics comics until I found the advertisement I remembered: "Self

Hypnosis Made Easy." A buck ninety-five. I had to vow on the tiny order from that I was over nineteen. No problem. Who would check to see if I was lying? Three weeks later I was in business. I was on the verge of magnificent heights of attainment.

I studied the text carefully. I learned how to relax every part of my body. Even the parts that I didn't know I had. You were to silently say things to yourself like this:

"You are beginning to relax your entire body. You are feeling relaxed. The relaxation begins in your feet. In your toes. It moves up into the small of your foot. Then into the heel. Now the relaxation is moving into your ankles and your calf. Feel the relaxation. Next you are to relax your knees. Feel the relaxation in your kneecaps and then your lower thighs. Now your upper thighs. Now the relaxation is spreading in your groin and surrounding your buttocks . . ." Believe me it took a while to get used to silently naming all those odds and ends. Sometimes I'd crack up just thinking about relaxed buttocks, but I was determined to master the fine art of self-hypnosis.

Eventually you got around to relaxing your head — your mouth, eyes, ears, lips, skull, and penultimately the brain. Then you count backwards ten to one and you are deep in self-hypnosis. In fact, when I first tried it, I was so damn deep inside my subconscious that it just gave up all together and told me to fall asleep. But after a few tries, I got the hang of not falling asleep. I'd go into my self-hypnotic trance with certain self-improving instructions because, by now, I was up to lesson thirteen in the book: "How to Bring About Self-improvement."

I started with something easy. Maybe I wouldn't pick my nose in public again. No, something greater, something more substantial. I told myself I was going to ace the math test tomorrow. I repeated it over and over, then fell asleep.

Sure enough, I aced the math test. Son of a bitch.

Next I told myself I would actually *like* school. I wouldn't dread it so much. I wouldn't mind getting up in the morning —

in the dark, dismal depths of winter — to trudge off through the gray, soggy snowdrifts to sit in boring classes where teachers shouted unnecessary insults at you and fellow students did the same later in the playground.

It took me three nights' work but I did it. I got up in the unlit coal mine of a 6:30 winter morning, slogged off to school and started hurling abuse back at teachers and peers alike. As a direct result, I actually started to like school. Sure, my grades began to slip because of my new found rudeness but I felt so much more at home. I felt self-improved.

I didn't tell anyone what I was up to. My mother would have called it witchcraft. And I did have this deep-seated fear that maybe I was in over my head. I had lied about being nineteen. Maybe if an eleven-year-old practiced self-hypnosis it did something terrible to his brain cells. But eleven is an age where everything that seems fun or meaningful is already labelled as bad for you. So I wasn't about to quit.

The big test was ahead of me. I would succeed at getting Jeannie Strauss to like me, nay, to fall in love with me. Exactly how self-hypnosis (of me) would do this I didn't know. But the need was clear. I relaxed every muscle in my body, dropped into my substrata of thought processes, and went to work. It seemed I had convinced myself I was going deeper and deeper into the depths each time I went under.

What if I couldn't pull myself back? I wondered. What if I lost it altogether? In the day, the fear would collect like old mayonnaise in my brain but, at night, I pressed on into the Amazon of the sub-conscious. Three days had passed and nothing had worked with Jeannie. I again queried the logic of how hypnotizing me could effect Jeannie. And then, she smiled at me. It was from afar, but it was a smile.

Then she talked to me. Out of the blue. And then she wrote me a little note during social studies. I had done it. Mind over matter. I pressed on at night re-affirming my mission and my success. We had achieved a week-long, healthy relationship of note passing. Her handwriting was beautiful. Mine was a scrawl. I'd have to work on that later along with other minor tidbits of self-improvement: looks, athletic ability, etc. I was a skinny little kid and wanted to gain muscle and weight and agility. Certainly, if hypnosis had attained my Jeannie, I could accomplish just about anything else that was on my list.

And then suddenly, for no apparent reason, Jeannie stopped sending notes to me and started passing them to Ray Forbes. I tried better handwriting, bigger words, more complex sentiments . . . for up till now we had corresponded mostly about how ugly our teachers were and how much we "liked" each other. I'll still never forget how she had inscribed, "I like you more, I think, than I liked Roger or Greg last year."

But then came Ray and she liked Ray even more than me, or so she admitted in her final, quadra-folded epistle. Self-hypnosis would not bring her back. Whatever Ray Forbes had, it was more powerful than my sub-conscious. So I grew sullen again. I stopped relaxing the small of my feet and my buttocks and I went back to being the unimproved me.

For years afterwards, self-improvement was hard to come by. I worked things out the hard way through my conscious, often unwilling mind. And it wasn't until Barry Konicov sent me his promotions package that I thought that, yes, maybe now was the time to go after a modified me. I could choose something, perhaps, from the "Success Series": "Positive Thinking," maybe. Or "Developing Enthusiasm." "Goal Setting" would be a good one as would "How To Be Popular." No, too reminiscent of my attempts with Jeannie. "Imagining" sounded interesting.

"More than 40% of us have not developed our ability to imagine. I used to be in this category. Now I can picture with the best of them. Even my dreams are in color," a successful graduate of this tape attested. It would be like moving up from an old fifteen-inch black and white to a contemporary twenty-eight-inch color monitor," I figured.

It sounded easy enough. Run the self-hypnosis side at

night, hearing the actual words and then, in the day — "even while you are driving!" — listen to the other side. All you would consciously hear would be waves lapping on a shoreline. (That's all I hear many days where I live anyway . . . but not to worry.) Imbedded in the sound of waves would be subliminal messages. I wouldn't even be aware that I'd be learning things.

What happened if you accidentally flipped on the self-hypnosis side while driving? I wondered. Would I think I was a chicken or see UFOS or simply relax myself into a fiery auto-motive death?

But it wasn't the self-hypnosis side that worried me. It was the side where I heard only waves. I would be learning while I wasn't learning. Spooky. How could I be one hundred percent sure that Potentials Unlimited weren't screwing around with the inner me? Suppose balding, smiling Barry Konicov, Chairman of the Board of Potentials, was out to turn me into something worse than a UFO watcher or a chicken? Suppose it was a conniving plot to turn Americans into Republicans. (For what else could possibly explain those last ten years of mindlessness?) Or what if he was ready to take over the world?

Given the advertised opportunities, however, I was thinking that maybe I should take the chance. It was an impressive list of titles like "Overcoming Procrastination," "Subconscious Sales Power." And even the metaphysical stuff — "Astral Projection," "Past Life Regression with Mate or Lover," "Remote Viewing," and "Aura Reading." On the health side there were: "Freedom from Acne," and "Arthritis Pain Relief," and even "Get More Joy Out of Sex (Male or Female Version)." What if you accidentally got one with the wrong label? I wondered. And of course, my favorites, "Freedom from Disappointment," as well as "Healthy Teeth and Gums," and "Overcoming Jet Lag."

I wanted them all. I read all 32 pages. Already I felt like a new man. I was hopeful as I had been at age eleven. I decided that this wasn't just a hokum mass-mail appeal. The tapes were only six bucks each. For maybe a hundred smackers you could make a major personality inroad. For three- hundred clams you might have a whole new life ahead of you with wealth and healthy teeth and gums to boot. If you bought the entire set, I figured you could probably correct world problems in areas of poverty, war, and food shortage while freeing yourself from guilt and astral projecting all over the place at the same time.

And then I remembered. Potentials had actually sent me a tape. A free sample I was too excited to even read the label. I rushed to the Sanyo and popped it in. As promised, nothing but waves. Fake waves, I think. They were too regular. It sounded nice but I think it was the old counterfeit white noise drifting in and out. It was comforting though, so I listened for maybe twenty minutes. What did I feel afterwards? What was the message? I couldn't pin it down. Okay, I said, it was only one shot. Turn it over, listen to the self-hypnosis side, find out what self-improvement I was working on. I listened.

"This is the self-hypnosis side of the tape. Do not listen to it while driving. You are about to begin a program of weight loss. Soon you will lose the pounds you so richly deserve to lose. You are feeling very relaxed. The relaxation begins in your toes and it moves into the small of your feet . . ."

I stood up and snapped off the machine. *Weight loss.* At thirty-eight years old I still weighed one hundred and thirty-eight pounds. I hadn't gained anything since I was maybe fifteen years old. What a quirk of fate. Or what a cruel joke played on me by Potentials Unlimited. What was going on down there in Michigan? Had they failed to read my aura or have a flunky astrally project up here to Nova Scotia to see which tape I would have found interesting. Shoot.

Now I realized that I wasn't hungry. I eat often and a lot; now, suddenly, for no apparent reason, I was not hungry. The ocean side, the subliminal side, had already made inroads. In a week I would be anorexic, within a month, starved to death. I'd have no more of it. I got up and went to the refrigerator for a beer and a sandwich. I tried to undo the damage as best I could.

Maybe in another twenty-six years I'd try self-hypnosis and the subliminal again. But right now I felt too young, too impressionable and vulnerable. I decided again that I was happy with my own life. My habits, happiness, and neurosis. All of the untested tapes would have to wait: "Be a Better Bowler," "Stop Being Angry," and "Recapture Youth and Vigor." I had learned before that the sub-conscious is not to be trusted. Some things I'd just have to work out the old fashioned way.

20

Spiritual Wrestling in Woolco

I am a congenital non-shopper. I hate stores and shopping malls and in general dislike the addictive practice of buying anything. Today I am up against a Himalayan task. I am about to spend two and one half hours inside a Woolco store. I won't permit myself to set foot beyond the threshold of this mercantile kingdom until my time is up. There is no way around it. I have challenged myself to this feat in the way that a sixty-year-old Tibetan guru might set before himself the task of walking a hot bed of coals. I want to prove to myself that I am in control of my mind. There's no other way.

The scene is the Penhorn Mall in suburban Dartmouth. The word *Penhorn* refers to chickens. Not far from here was a massive chicken ranch. Once this neighborhood smelled pervasively of chicken guano and singed feathers. Now a shopping mall, salvaged twice from bankruptcy, nests upon the asphalt parking lot like a grotesque squatting concrete and steel leghorn. Or penhorn, as the case may be.

The tread on my car tires has worn thin. And Woolco has a

165

sale on all-season radials. The lure is too much. I'm about to be sucked into the store of linoleum aisles and incessant florescent lights. Perhaps it's a trap. Perhaps it is my destiny.

I ease the station wagon into the automotive service bay and jockey it into position for the hydraulic hoist. The garage door begins to close of its own accord behind me. It falls from the ceiling in a controlled vertical drop until its rubber skirt is kissing oil-stained concrete. There is no turning back now.

A car mechanic looks at my two front tires. One is bald and showing tiny metal wires — what's left of the steel belting. The other tire is still showing hieroglyphs of a tread. "Save that one for me, okay?" I ask the mechanic for I am not a man of waste.

The mechanic can tell he's up against a no-nonsense car owner. I'm not going to be fooled. "I ain't never seen a tire worn down to the steel belt before," he says, admiring the unsalvageable one. I beam proudly and wonder if there might be any warranty credit left on a tire with a good one hundred thousand kilometers under its belt.

I watch as he removes the front wheels, studies the grooves on the brake disks. He pops a brake pad and shows me clean, shiny iron where asbestos should be. "Okay," I say, "brakes all around."

Then we notice the dripping gasoline. The gas line from the tank to the engine is leaking like an automatic coffee drip machine. The shop manager walks over, flicks some glowing ashes from his cigarette toward the puddle of gas accumulated onto the floor. "I'd have that taken care of too, if I was you," he advises, shrewd beyond belief.

"Yes," I concede, "that too."

I spin my sole credit card around in the dark reaches of my imagination. An estimate is given . . . something that sounds like a down-payment on a condominium. But I have been negligent toward my car. Worse than the cost, however, is the time estimate. Two and one half hours. The weather is against me today. There's rain and a driving east wind. "Why not just walk around the store for a while?" the manager says. "Shop or something."

I nod in blind confusion. My brain is already going numb. *Shop*. Two and one half hours, maybe more . . . wandering around inside the Penhorn Woolco, the worst of eleven possible nightmares coming alive before my eyes. The names of the hours stretch out before me like eras of geological time. Ten-thirty is a vague rumor. Eleven-thirty no more than a failing hope. Twelve noon is light years away.

I stumble off into the store. A buzzer is sounding to release the door that shuttles me into the mercantile kingdom. And suddenly I am there. Awash in life-draining florescent lights. The auto department is filled with chrome-plated lug nut covers and an infinity of car waxes. A Kraco car radio is cranked up, and Ann Murray sounds like she is singing inside a cement mixer.

At first, all hope seems lost. Should I fend my way through the jungle of merchandise to the far end of the store and wander out into the mall? Try on shoes, look for remainders in Classics books? Fondle the vegetables in the Sobeys Food Village? Make acquaintance with the banking machine or talk to the travel agent? What?

Then it comes to me. This moment was meant to be. I need to smile in the face of adversity, turn this crisis into a test of will. What did Blake say: "Truth is anything the mind can conceive?" And the human mind has framed Woolco into existence. Why not confront the whole textural fabric of this place? Why not observe and record, try to understand this thing that so befuddles me? I sense immediately that I am on the track to some form of enlightenment. Flash cubes are popping in the neuro-circuits of my brain. I am in the belly of the beast, I say to myself. I must watch out for the acids that might digest me, the demons that might come from behind room fresheners and freeze-dried peanuts. But I will seek out large truths inside this store.

I start with books. There are two rows; nothing sells for list. There is an adventure in bad literature here. I fear that someday I will discover one of my own books here, remaindered and selling three for ninety-nine cents. But not today. I am not that successful of a failure yet. However, I do find one good book: *Giving Good Weight* by John McPhee. $2.98. McPhee is a master wordsmith. I'll buy it. What the hell does the title mean? I take it back to the Woolco Grill with me, unpurchased. I buy a magnificently large cup of coffee for less than a dollar. It's the size of a small child's swimming pool. The styrofoam alone is worth a quarter. This is the kind of coffee that a trucker would appreciate. Truckers have tubes that suck in coffee intravenously, then the tubes suck it back out and pollute the highways even as they drive.

I am sitting in the grill with my massive cup of coffee, reading. McPhee, a journalist, a recorder of human life and whimsy is good. I'm inspired to write myself. I look around, caffeine flooding my veins, my eyesight enhanced as if I had just swallowed some hallucinatory drug. First I see the tiny crumpled metal ashtray before me with cigarettes, lipstick stains right up to the final burn line. Around me is a sea of faces, all looking like they've just been propped up out of the coffin . . . it must be the damn lighting. At the Woolco Grill, I discover, you can buy a dish of fake, aerosol-whipped cream for $1.25.

Some employees are behind me, gossiping. I overhear this: "It's a thin store today." *Thin;* that means not very crowded. And another answers, "It's K-Mart Days. That always happens." The competition. Now they are discussing what is on sale in K-Mart. Here are people who live their lives inside Woolco and in their off hours, they roam the aisles of the major competition. Clearly it's a way of life.

Once I finish gulping the coffee, I pick up McPhee and go in search of the next essentials. I need a pen and a notebook. I want to write this all down before it gets away. I fight my way through glassware trying to find the stationery section, get distracted by some highly polished "pilsner" beer glasses. Suddenly, I want a set of them. I can see golden beer flowing, filling them to the brim. Instead, I duck my head down, like a charging bull and roar past. A pen and a notebook, nothing else.

Up ahead there is a woman with a shopping cart staring at a headless, chestless, plastic torso of a man (lopped off at the knees) who is wearing nothing more than a pair of black jockey briefs. Her shopping cart is half-filled with junk food and bathroom items. She is just standing, transfixed, staring at the underwear. This is a dangerous place, I remind myself.

I find a row of pens. I study the prices, examine the quality. Nothing seems to suit. I wanted something for a quarter, but I can tell they wouldn't feel right. I'm a professional writer, after all, a man who needs a good, serviceable pen. BIC is not what it used to be. Venus is tempting but poorly designed. I settle for a black plastic Papermate: 72 cents. It occurs to me what I am doing. I'm shopping. God help me.

I ask McPhee what to do. The book stares dumbly back : *Giving Good Weight.* (Is the title sexual? I didn't think so.) Now I need a notebook, a simple task. I only want paper, for Christ sake. That shouldn't be so hard.

Steno notebooks don't feel right in my paw. They are for people who understand the inner secrets of shorthand. There's nothing left but the sort of notebooks that high-school students use and all are overpriced. I find nothing suitable for recording even Woolco epiphanies. This is terrible. I almost give up but remember my quest. I settle for a $2.50 small notebook with an airbrush reproduction of a 1957 Corvette. The notebook has a name: *'57 Heaven.* What the hell.

I remember that kids call these "scribblers." Other children of the world call them notebooks. Canadians call them scribblers. *Ipso facto,* Canadian children scribble where other youth spend their time taking notes. I save this morsel for later consideration. The book is manufactured by, who else, Hilroy. There is not a notebook on the shelf that is not a Hilroy. Perhaps there is not a notebook in Canada that is not Hilroy. Hilroy, who ever he may be, must have a massive grip on the scribbler market in Canada. I don't like the implications. Now, however, I find I like the weight of '57 *Heaven* in my hands. My mind has already locked onto the thrill of the wire coil and the empty, potential pages. I realize I will feel a great sense of loss if I put Mr. Hilroy's product back on the shelf.

I wonder if I should go back to the grill and begin to write with my unpurchased pen and my unpurchased notebook. Would that be, in its own way, shoplifting? As the thought enters my brain, I look over my shoulder to see a young male with a very formal demeanor staring me, then turning away quickly to check the price on some typewriter correction fluid. They're on to me now. They know I am not a *regular shopper*. From here on, I'll have to be careful lest I lose my courage or even find myself arrested.

I begin a zig-zag in the direction of the checkout register, try to shake the snoop who is on my tail. He hangs back, dodges down a side aisle of multicolored filing cabinets and luggage. My attention is turned to my environs again, the wonder and the glory of the multiplicity of Things.

Since I don't usually shop, I never knew that such stuff existed. I venture far and wide. First, it's back toward automotive, to look longingly through the glass door at my hoisted car, then a brief love affair with imitation leather steering wheel covers. I admire the new propane safety shut off valves for gas barbecue. And then, without warning, I'm up against a large display of salad spinners. Other shoppers are admiring them, too.

"There really is nothing quite like a dry salad," says one matron reaching for the item.

"Once you spin a salad, there's no going back," her friend says.

Over the P.A. comes a message from the bored voice of a novice reader. "Shoppers, don't miss out on 40% off on our ladies' hosiery for the next hour." Didn't I just hear on the news that Oliver North spent a large chunk of his payment for the Iran-Contra arms deal on hosiery? Too bad Ollie was not here with me today.

Before, I was oblivious to the P.A. system. Now I hear everything, even the Muzak. It had been there all along and I had never noticed. A Hundred and One Strings plays the Rolling Stones. Trumpet versions of old Monkees songs and several hundred variations of "Tie a Yellow Ribbon Round the Old Oak Tree." I begin to drown in it. Fortunately, the music is punctuated more often now, as the morning grows old, with proclamations of special offers. They have borrowed from Walt Whitman who once said, "To you, endless announcements."

I walk at a faster clip. I want to see and hear everything. Fragments of conversation rocket past me. People say, "Huh?" a lot to each other. One shopper remarks, "That's cheap," while fondling a synthetic sweater. I hear an outraged patron burst, "A dollar ninety-five," at a plastic earring display.

Why am I still thinking about that steering wheel cover? Perhaps it is something I have needed for a long time. Why have I been depriving myself? I go back and pick it up.

In the pet section, the parakeets are lively and noisy. I would like to take one home. And the Max Headroom Skateboards . . . I'm not too old to appreciate a nice set of polyurethane wheels and a custom kicktail.

Plastic eavestroughing. Just snap it together. Now that's a snazzy idea. Video games are going for only ninety-nine cents now. I always despised video games and I don't have anything to play them on but I feel nearly obliged to take advantage of this sensational offer. It's almost like they're giving merchandise away!

I stop back at the grill, scribble some notes quickly before it all slides away from me. I'm in luck. Two men are setting up a twenty-foot step ladder to change the light in the ceiling. Aside from the cursing, the work is sheer Woolco ballet. The eventual folding of the ladder is a masterpiece of diligence.

Reeling, with only an hour to go, I return to the trek. There is a fabulous car-washing device that could improve the quality of my life and free up my time for better things. Compact disc players are displayed and described as "essential." And the kitchen gadgets department is a place of the imagination. Bar novelty glasses with stupid jokes. Nude women ice cube makers. Twelve different types of shish kebab kits. Electric potato chippers and vegetable "roto-cutters."

Then it's on to multi-colored shoe laces, endless plastic sandals, tube socks, bow ties, vast numbers of Planters Peanut jars, dayglo light switches, a device that turns the average electric drill into a manufacturing plant.

I ricochet from one department to the next. There are enough plastic guns in the toy department to stage a coup in a minor republic. From behind a He Man and the Masters of the Universe coloring book, I see a familiar face. The floorwalker has been keeping up with me. He wonders what the hell I am up to with my frenetic searching and note-taking. Perhaps I am a spy from the competition, he wonders. I smile politely.

I have grown high on the wonders of the store. I've got a buzz on from the eclectic excitement of endless products. I no longer care about my car. I just want to cruise these aisles until I have fingered everything, until I have compared every price and product. There is a pair of black Levi pants on a table in men's wear. I had a pair like these once when a teenager. Those pants were a part of an entire new image and mind dimension for me. On the third washing, my mother (purposefully perhaps) poured in Chlorox bleach and my image was dashed on the rocks of despair. Now, I will buy a new pair, and repair my psyche.

Woolco has reached deep into my mind and inserted fishhooks. Perhaps I should get out quick before they reel me in. But the fever is growing.

At length, however, I have circumnavigated the store and

spiralled in toward the very heart of the ultra-discount tables. Smiley Bates and Slim Whitman albums are a dollar ninety-five in Records. Pee Wee Herman videos are for sale nearby. But finally I find myself in an aisle with nothing but yarn. Two grand-mothers are discussing the pros and cons of various shades of pink angora yarn. I stare at the yarn skeins and the absolute boredom of all that fuzziness begins to undo the drug of the store.

I look at the goods I am clutching to my chest. What have I become? I ask myself silently.

The voice comes over the P.A.: "Woolco shoppers, Polish dill pickles are now on sale for one dollar and thirty-five cents in the front of the store. Choose from plain or spicy dill and for gherkin lovers . . ."

I rush to the front check-out line. I'll buy the steering wheel cover, the black Levis, the papermate pen, the McPhee text, and the Hilroy notebook. But that's it. No more.

After my purchase I weave my way back to the garage. The tires are balanced, the brakes are installed, the gas line leak repaired. The car is lowered. I've paid my money and I begin to drive off.

Outside, I see that shrubs are forty percent off in the outdoor garden department. I set the handbrake, get ready to leave the car. But just then, the heavens open up. I close the door again, restart the car. The rain begins to erase the Woolco from my vision. I feel myself returning to normal. I realize that I have survived my ordeal. The final count was two hours and forty-five minutes inside. My wife and friends will not believe me, but I have goods to show them. I may bear a few permanent scars but I can prove to them that I've been to the Penhorn and, alas, I have shopped.

21

Returning to America

New Jersey has a strong nar-
rative line. My life pivots
around this place. I was born there and return at least once a
year. Driving south from Nova Scotia, I feel the infection of
America slightly in Maine, then I tweak a higher temperature
on the abbreviated New Hampshire Turnpike. Massachusetts
and Connecticut create a fever, New York a madness, and by the
time I conclude the Tappan Zee Bridge and turn south into
New Jersey, I am somebody else again. I am the old me, the one
who lived there before leaving. I am delirious with a kind of
cluttered confusion at being re-introduced to the other one, the
stranger.

At the MacDonald's in Bucksport, Maine — an immaculate
little burger haven perched over a body of water — I read in *The
Bangor Times* that the U.S. would spend 299.5 billion dollars on
defence next year. This from a country that cannot afford
medical care for its own population. My wife and I argue over
how many zeros there are in a billion. I say it's a one followed by
eight zeros. She says nine. Later my mother will look it up for
me and I find I was wrong. A billion is a thousand million. If
you took 2,995 millionaires and had them donate all their

175

money to new weapons, officer's clubs and free airfare for soldiers, you'd be able to save the average taxpayer from having to foot the bill.

The numbers dance in my head for the remainder of my journey south to Jersey. I should not be surprised or staggered by any of this but I am. I want desperately to love the people and the place from where I came but, instead, I retreat into a mental cloud of anger.

Americans own so many things and spend so much time buying stuff that they miss out on a whole bunch of living. Why so much of everything? I keep asking them. The question is rhetorical. It feels good to consume. I could get swept up in it but I counter that I don't have enough time: 299.5 billion dollars keep swirling in my head. I want to (as usual) go looking for my past, looking for the heart and soul of New Jersey.

Davey Jones, one of the original Monkees, is staging a free performance at the Cherry Hill Mall. I try to get there in time but get caught in snarled traffic. Later I hear him on the radio. He's a reformed alcoholic. Rock and roll nearly wrecked him for life, this short little Brit who once sang the then-sensible line: "I wanna be free, like the bluebird high above me . . ."

Later still at a gathering of relatives, there's a car accident on Route 70. The highway was designed in the forties for high-speed rural travel. The community is now suburban. Cars still drive high speed, bumper to bumper. So scenes like this happen.

The Catholic church has just let out from a Saturday afternoon service. An old man is walking across the highway. Somebody's brakes don't work and he gets nailed. Blood on the old concrete. A handful of cars caught up in the after-effects are smashed and strewn on lawns and divider barriers. A few kids crying.

The lady who hit him has a head wound, tells the audience, "Nothing bad like this ever happens to me. This can't be real." Priests begin to wander about. Nuns are praying behind the bushes. Those who know how, offer help. Others worry about law suits. One man looks straight at me and shakes his head, "This society," he snarls.

The words echo in my head. He wants to place blame for accidents. We all want to do that. I'm almost afraid I understand what he means. But it can't be that easy.

I want to see this place in the days when it was as beautiful as Nova Scotia. In my childhood, it was almost that way. The forests had trees sixty feet high — oak, maple, beech, trees with trunks as thick as elephants. Streams ran clean and brimmed with frogs and fish. All gone to houses and warehouses and highways. My own lament can only be a cliché. Let it go.

My father has infinite patience. At sixty-two he stands as a kind of mystic in my family. Nothing phases him. Together we watch Bob Hope's fiftieth anniversary on ABC.

I go shopping at a giant used clothing store and spend seventy dollars. My wardrobe for two years to come. The great spin-off of such an excessive society is that you can always buy second-hand things at little expense. Dreams here are like cash flow. Only next year it is imperative to make more than this year. Otherwise you are on a decline. Headed toward the skids.

In the *Philadelphia Inquirer* is an article about the ratings of 250 jobs in America. Best to worst. Book author comes in at number 136 just above shipping clerk and teacher. We're all in the bottom third of lousy jobs. I have no complaints. Nuclear power plant decontamination technicians log in at 147, a mere 11 clicks down from me as a writer. Should this indicate something? But dig deeper and you find the real heartbreak. 193: Astronaut — a bum deal even though the press is good. My father and brother — both auto mechanics held down a 207 job, easily in the last 50. But further still: photojournalist at 223 (lots of getting beat-up and shot at); garbage collector at 226 (who knows what filth you gotta pick up these days?); and then from 241 down to the basement: pro football player, cowboy, lumberjack, roustabout, dairy farmer, seaman, roofer, construction worker, commercial fisherman, and finally, migrant worker.

The bottom ten is Jack London territory. Society is still resting firmly on the laborer who is busting his hump to keep the rest of us alive.

My uncle comes over for coffee to share a theory. "You know what's gonna happen one of these years, don't ya? The pink money."

"Pink money?" I ask.

"It's like in the army. One day you had this government issue money that was good, the next day it wasn't. And you'd have to trade in ten of your blue money for one of the pink money." He was thinking about the state of the economy, the debt.

"$299.5 billion for defence this year," I offer up for analysis.

"Sure," his hand launches into outer space. "And most of it is a waste."

I was surprised to find a sympathetic mind.

"Let Washington put it toward health care," I say. All around me in New Jersey I hear people worrying about how to survive old age without going broke, without languishing in some shabby public hospital bed. Middle class people are afraid they'll die beggars.

"What are you, crazy?" he says. "We wouldn't get any of it. It would all go to the poor." There's a fundamental fear of the poor still alive in the suburbs and "decent" sections of the city. I think of the thirties.

"It won't matter once they get out the pink money, anyway. Here's one pink for a thousand of your green. Wait, you'll see."

"But don't you feel the $299.5 billion is a bit high to spend on more bombs?"

"You bet it is," he agrees. "But if we didn't spend it, the Russians would come up with some new weapon and take us all over. What do you know about it? You're up there in Canada. We'll have to protect you if it comes to a war."

Thanks for the memories.

Later I find myself explaining my worries over all the American excess. I tell my mom about the women in the Kalahari that spend all day digging roots and bashing them, preparing them into something edible. It goes on day after day or they starve. My mother says she couldn't live like that.

The job ratings in the paper were based on salary, stress, work environment, outlook, security, and physical demands. In those terms, the fisherman and the migrant worker are completely screwed.

A letter to Dear Abby is from a woman in Texas who says that they now have a museum with live butterflies because most have died off in her section of the country due to pollutants in the air. She's upset. So is Abigail Van Buren. Sure, something can be done, they both argue.

When I self-righteously proclaim how individuals, not governments, will be responsible for disarming the world, people in New Jersey believe me to be completely insane. Almost all of them are very polite about it, though. They tolerate my eccentricity and offer me another barbecued hamburger. Almost none exhibit any interest in nuclear war. Prices of things, however, command continued discussion. Lawn furniture, gasoline, toys.

When was it during *your* life that you discovered that the country was being run by madmen? For me it came during the Vietnam War. I was in high school. I was upset because I had almost established a relationship with a girl I was in love with. Her name was Cherie. My big chance was at a friend's party. Cherie would be there. I would be there. We would both be thirteen years old and ready to dance together, to touch, to be ourselves and to find a corner with the lights turned off however briefly.

Only Cherie never showed up. Her friends would not tell me why. Some of them tried to be nice to me, danced with me. There was something I was not supposed to know.

I called Cherie the next day and learned that her brother had just been killed in Vietnam. I did a shitty job of trying to console her on the phone. I had never met her brother, but I was mad at him for getting killed. For screwing up my chance to get to know Cherie better, to have her as a girlfriend. I knew the opportunity would never happen now.

Over the next few days I made some emotional transfers. I stopped being angry at her brother. I got angry at the Viet Cong. And I started watching the TV news at six o'clock. I watched the war and then I listened to the speeches of Lyndon Johnson and then I thought some more about having lost my chance with Cherie and about Cherie's dead brother. And then suddenly it clicked. The United States of America was being run by a lunatic with the assistance of several other madmen.

While back visiting in New Jersey, I went with my mother and father to the Beverly National Cemetery. My grandfather was in the First World War, and when he died, the government gave him an American flag. He had always been a lover of American flags. Too bad, in fact, he wasn't still alive to see the one that now flies over the Village liquor store in Cinnaminson where he lived. It's the largest American flag I've ever seen, big enough to cover several building lots in my old home town that has developed from farmland to suburb to small city.

In the Beverly Cemetery, each grave was marked according to which war the deceased had fought in. Civil, Spanish American, WWI, WW II, Korea, Vietnam. My grandfather's flag was being donated back to the government so it would fly over the dead on holidays along with hundreds more. It was a kind of American flag heaven.

That summer there was a plague of ticks in South Jersey. I couldn't send my daughter out into the yard without her coming back with a couple of ticks hanging like jewelery to her ear lobes. Cattle egrets were the natural foragers of ticks and there were very few cattle egrets left in New Jersey because there were very few cattle free to roam the fields anymore because there were no more fields. Toxins and pollutants didn't bother the ticks and they were having a great summer. I ended up bringing a few back to Nova Scotia, hidden in the thick black fur of my dog. Vaseline, oil, and even lit matches wouldn't free the buggers. I pulled one out with needle nose pliers but the blasted heads stayed rooted in the skin. Nearly a month later I had to dig them out with a sharp knife. The ticks of New Jersey die hard.

Each time I go back, I understand less about the place. I live in a fairy-tale world, a sanctuary that may exist for the rest of my life. Maybe not.

It was also the summer when the public learned that the evangelists were having a great time in bed with young women who were not their wives. And it was the summer that candidates were looking for nominations to be president, then vying for presidency. The candidates were all men, no women. One of them was black but everyone knew he'd not be elected or if he was, he'd be shot soon enough.

It was toward the end of the summer that George Bush put his hand over his heart and began to recite the pledge of allegiance often in public. His opponent suddenly seemed somehow less American simply because *he* didn't do the same. Bush's popularity soared. And therein lay the crude hard truth.

The myth of America supercedes any fact, any crime and any logic. The price is high — $299.5 billion is a drop in the bucket up against the 3 trillion dollar debt. And none of us know how many zeroes there are in trillion. Besides, Americans have lived through all kinds of inflation before. Dreams die hard.

22

In Search of a President

I now have something in common with Art Linkletter. Neither one of us can be president of the United States. It comes as the most recent in a long string of poignant realizations that mark this phase of my adult male masculine development.

I remember learning as a child that Art could not become president because he had not been born in America. Something like that. He was an immigrant and did funny, warm and corny shows with normal people on TV before normal people on television were entirely replaced by people who had some incredibly unusual quality . . . like tap dancing on the seat of a rolling unicycle, that sort of thing. I'm an immigrant in the opposite direction from Art. I moved to Canada, and even though I haven't ever denounced outright my American citizenship, I expect the American public would have a hard time electing a president who has spent the last ten years in Canada. I could offer a hundred good explanations as to how I had been preparing for the oval office and why, in order to be the quintessential American, it was important to live outside of the borders for a number of years to shore up my own unique Americanness.

But I don't think any of the major parties will ask me to run. I will, however, fill out an absentee ballot in November and write in my own name for president. Just this once. Just for the record. I'll write in my wife's name for VP. We'd make a great team. Or maybe I should probably reverse it. My wife has far more common sense than I do. But I'd be afraid it would go to her head. Either way, if elected, we would probably make several sweeping changes in America. Socialized medicine, for example. No Star Wars. Fix up the parks in the cities. Stop poisoning pigeons. Do away with nuclear weapons and change the drapes in the White House. The whole decor would be changed over to goods bought in Woolco and K Mart. We'd move the capitol to Ocracoake Island off the coast of North Carolina just to avoid the bureaucrats. Let them stay in D.C.

But my guess is that the county clerk back in New Jersey who will count the absentee ballots will see only one vote for the Choyces. I don't even know if I can get my wife to go along with voting for me or herself. She'll opt for someone whose name is already printed on the ballot. I can handle that sort of domestic rebellion.

Recognizing that the likelihood of me being swept to power as a dark horse candidate was decidedly slim, I thought I should do some research to improve my chances. The year was 1988. Americans were gearing up for a presidential election and I was home in New Jersey. There was a primary coming up there in June and candidates were campaigning in the state. Michael Dukakis was going to be in Camden, about fifteen minutes from my parents' suburban home. My mother had heard it on KYW Action News.

I grabbed a notebook, borrowed my father's car, and went looking for the man who had a better shot at the oval office than I did. He was to be in North Camden, Jesse Jackson territory, giving a news conference at a community daycare center in one of the roughest parts of that small industrial city across the river from Philadelphia. It was May 16, 1988. I tried phoning all the numbers in the phone book that would lead me into the labyrinths of the Democratic Party machine for Camden County, but for each new number I phoned, the line was held down by someone who answered, "Jesse Jackson for President." I wanted the exact location of the Dukakis conference but no one would tell me.

After phoning a local congressman, I finally got a line with someone who owned up to the fact that he worked for Dukakis. "How did you get this number?" he asked. It appeared to be a closely guarded secret.

I explained I was a Canadian journalist and had got the number from Congressman Florio's office. "No one is supposed to know this number," he said, but he proceeded to send me on to the news conference anyway. I learned I had only ten minutes to get there.

My father had grave doubts about sending his Buick and his son into such a rough neighborhood. Fear of places like Camden runs very deep in the suburbs of New Jersey. Only bad news ever came out of Camden. My father didn't like the idea of losing his son and his Buick on the same day. But he saw I was intent. I think he silently prayed that at least one of us would come out of it unscathed.

So I drove off in search of Dukakis. What was I looking for? I wanted to see a presidential campaign in action. Dukakis was in enemy territory. Later the press would call it a "high risk visit to a Jesse Jackson stronghold." Maybe the guy was okay. He appeared spry and elfin on TV; there was just a hint of Kennedy about him to entice the public. He was in favor of socialized medicine and trimming the military budget. I had seen him rated in a *MS* magazine survey that I had read on an airplane. *MS* liked him. I think I did too.

As I drove south on Route 130 to Camden, I assumed my Canadian reporter persona. I did want to get into the press conference and I was, after all, a writer. I drove on toward State Street.

Camden. Home of Walt Whitman. Home of RCA and Campbell's Soup. In the old days, the Delaware River would run blood red when they were making the soup from Jersey tomatoes. People couldn't swim in the river in the early part of the century during processing time. It would be a river of soupy, pulpy tomato flesh and blood coursing out to the sea. That was before the flush of chemical waste killed the river for good.

Camden. I had given a poetry reading there at the Walt Whitman International Poetry Center on a Friday night early in my career. No one had shown up but a security guard and the guy who ran the place. Not even my relatives were willing to go into Camden on a Friday night. "What are you, crazy?" they all said.

Flashback: Camden, circa 1969. I was sitting in a basement coffeehouse on the Rutgers campus with my girlfriend listening to some laid-back Cajun music sung by a chubby white guy. Ten street toughs came in through the door and started threatening people. They smacked some chains on a table. We were so mellow in those days that we were hardly startled at first. Nobody could figure out exactly what the tough guys wanted. Money? Women? They stood guard by the only entrance into the basement. We were trapped, held like hostages. One well-meaning hippy among us tried to "talk them down," invited them to sit through the next set. The guy on stage even started singing again . . . "I went a fishin' to make a little money, so me and Angelina could have a little fun . . ." but the chain walloped down on the table again.

So eventually, before anybody really got hurt, some cops came and the troublemakers ran off. The gang leaders never did explain to us what was happening. The most they had done was shove a few pacifists up against the wall, the pacifists responding with, "Be cool, be cool. Hey, we're not, like, into violence, man."

Afterwards, I felt a bit shaken. I had held hard on to my girlfriend's hand and tried to keep her (and me) calm through the whole thing. I didn't understand inner city violence at all. I decided then that Camden was a frightening place.

I turned off Route 130 and found my way on State Street. The last time I had been in this part of town, North Camden, it was to sell a load of old newspaper and junk metal to a scrap dealer. I had my old '57 Chevy station wagon filled to the gunnels and had to drive up on a scale to get weighed before and after. I was a teenage junkman by profession, still hoping to be an astronaut or a president. With twelve bucks in my pocket for a load of scrap metal and old newspapers, I believed that all things were still possible. I was seventeen. Maybe I'd be an astronaut *and* a president. In either order.

But now. I was driving my father's Buick into a neighborhood that looked distinctly like another world. Abandoned buildings. People walking the streets throttling pit bull terriers and dobermans. The closer I go to my destination, the more alien it looked. It was an impossible place to live. Trashed furniture was everywhere. Whole living rooms seemed to exist in empty lots. Broken glass of all colors bloomed in the backyards. Windows were boarded up or windows were shattered. Not too much in between. What life went on inside these skeletal buildings would be hard to imagine. A corner park had grown deep in weeds and junked kitchen cabinets. Everything had been thrown away on the street. It was like the buildings had been pulled inside out. Whatever had happened here had happened years ago. The place had been forgotten by the suburbanites, the politicians, and even the charitable. If the media showed this place it would be to provide details about a murder or drugs on the street. This section of the city was reported to be the worst drug neighborhood in South Jersey. Most of the families in Cherry Hill, Cinnaminson, and the surrounding towns didn't want to be reminded that they lived ten miles from West Beirut.

The only good news to come out of Camden in recent years was that they had built a new maximum security prison at the foot of State Street. It provided some jobs and cut down on travel costs for criminals. Plans were afoot for an aquarium at the edge of the river, however. Everyone was hoping that a giant building full of expensive fish would help revive Camden. Anything would be worth a try.

I saw the blocked-off street, the idling Greyhound, a swarm of state policemen and a very ethnic crowd of onlookers. I parked on a side street, got out, and locked the car. I noticed that I had parallel parked amidst a string of cars all missing doors and headlights. Windshields were in various mosaics of shattered safety glass. I silently walked a block to the presidential campaign.

Outside of the R.E.S.P.O.N.D. community action centre stood trench coats and uniforms. The street had been cordoned off. Jesse Jackson banners flapped in the drizzly breeze. TV trucks sat idling on the sidewalks as street dogs weaved in and out between the legs of reporters. There were no presidential candidates on the street. I approached a state trooper and said I'd like to be permitted into the press conference. I was a writer from Nova Scotia in Canada.

There was something about the name Nova Scotia that made the trooper's eyebrows twitch. Maybe it was the overall foreignness of the sound. I don't know. I instinctively looked around at the rooftops: men perched up there with walky talkies circled the skyline.

"Do you have any I.D.?" I was asked.

What he wanted was a press card but I was hard up in that department, the bane of the freelancer. I showed my university I.D. My Nova Scotia driver's license (he examined the texture of the paper closely) and, realizing that suspicion was only growing thicker, I showed him my Visa card. Maybe that would somehow make me seem legitimate. It was a stupid move; it tipped them off that I was less than professional, probably a fool or a madman.

Why had I showed them my credit card? I stood rooted to

the sidewalk with the crowd around us while two policemen scrutinized my damn Visa card. Did they think it was a bribe? Maybe I was really in trouble now. Maybe this was the way bribes were handled now in Jersey. Police carried around little credit card machines and wrote in the amount. What the hell did I know about American progress? I'd been away a long time.

"That won't do you much good here," the incorruptible trooper said, handing me back all my credentials.

"Can I go in to the press conference?"

"Maybe later," he said, treating me as if I was eight years old. It meant no. "Go stand over there."

I went to stand beside a photographer from Oslo who had also been denied entrance. We were a small clot of foreign press. He snapped photos for his magazine back in Norway while I took notes. We never were let in. The small building was sealed up tight with Secret Service and cops. Only the day before a White supremacist couple from the Midwest had been foiled in a plot to assassinate Jesse Jackson. Security was tightening up on the presidential race everywhere. I sucked in the atmosphere on the street. Old women wheeling shopping carts. Dogs running everywhere. Not a Dukakis supporter in the crowd unless they had come on the bus.

I talked to a Hispanic looking group of guys, asked them what they thought was happening. "Must be Jesse Jackson in there," one said.

Dukakis was invisibly inside. If you hadn't seen the bus pull up, you wouldn't know he was there. Most people on the street thought it was Jesse. Who else would have the gall to come into North Camden? This was very interesting. Jesse Jackson was everywhere. He was even making an appearance when he wasn't even in the neighborhood. The ultimate presidential candidate.

I tried to convince them that it was Michael Dukakis, but they didn't believe me. The rain began to let up and the scene seemed to lighten. The cops started petting the dogs. People with suits and ties on who had come on the bus started to sip coffee. Nobody ever let me in the building and I could envision a long afternoon in a sealed room with an unshaven secret service man, so I didn't try any tricks to get in to see Dukakis. I wanted to ask him one question. I wanted to ask him, "What would you do about the 63,000 nuclear weapons on the planet?" It would have seemed out of place at the Camden press conference, I know. It was a place to talk daycare and war on drugs. If I lived in this neighborhood, I'd have a hard time worrying about nuclear war myself. Day-to-day survival would be enough. This looked like a place where no one had enough to get by and feel good about it.

The paradox hit me again about life in New Jersey. It was like a rude slap in the face. Everyone *I knew* in this state had too much. Too much money, too many toys, too many possessions. The night before I had eaten at a restaurant with my family, a place called the Golden Coral. We all ate too much food. There was too much available on the salad bar, the dessert bar, and the ice cream bar. We wasted too much. And now this. North Camden in the drizzle.

The story goes that people who lived there deserve it because they don't know any different. What would Michael Dukakis or any other president be able to do for them?

I walked back toward the car. There were three black guys standing by the Buick. When they saw me coming, they said something to each other and began running in three directions. One young man was headed straight toward me. At first I thought he was jogging. Then I decided he was zeroing in on me. I had turned a corner and was out of sight of the army of state troopers. I held tight onto the key in my pocket, saw the two others circling around in a wide, shallow arc. One yelled something to the other. I remembered Camden, 1969. And I was scared.

Ten feet from the car, still walking like nothing was bothering me. All I had to do was get the key in the door, hop in and lock it. Too late, the jogger was right in my path, he was bouncing on the balls of his feet, and running in place.

"What you need man? Whatever it is we got it."

I said nothing.

"C'mon man, what you need?"

"Nothing right now, thank you," I said. "Thanks anyway."

He spun on his shoes and disappeared down behind the row house. The other two were gone as well. *Nothing right now, thank you.* I had responded as if a waitress had just asked if I wanted another cup of coffee. All the while my heart was pounding. I felt relaxed enough to realize that for several seconds I had just felt a very real surge of adrenalin as the fear had gripped my gut.

I opened the Buick door, sat down, locked the door, and looked around at the streets that the news people called a "drug lord battleground." I thought about kids growing up here, the young man who wanted to know what I needed. I needed to see something change. I needed to need less than what I had and wanted to be able to share the skill. Maybe a new president would be good for Camden, even if it wasn't Jesse Jackson. Jesse's problem was that too many white Americans were scared stiff of having a Black president, of losing the power of all those white men in Washington.

Maybe Dukakis would bring high tech to State Street. Somebody would open up a computer software company on the corner; there'd be a microchip lab behind the daycare center. Some day there would be a MacDonald's here and it would be safe to go into the washroom without being mugged. I had failed in my attempt to interview the candidate but felt good to leave North Camden alive.

I drove around in circles at first trying to get a feel for the city, but I didn't get out of the car. Back on the highway, I drove straight to my parents' house. I passed only one real accident on the highway and had a single near-collision myself as I made my way back. Nothing grim enough to appear on the nightly news. On the highway, the cars were packed tight — three across, thousands deep, and driving along at fifty miles an hour. Later that night I saw Dukakis in his press conference. No one asked him about the 63,000 nuclear weapons. When asked how he would grab votes in New Jersey cities like Camden, he quipped, "with charisma." A shot outside the interview showed an aging black woman standing behind a "Win Jesse Win" banner. When asked about how she felt about Dukakis coming into the neighborhood, she looked away from the camera and said, "Hell, it's a free country. The man should be allowed to go wherever he likes."

23

Love Cuts Deep

The year was 1961, some-where in the middle of nine-teenth century. It was a year that I was prone to fits of falling in and out of love without ever discussing it with the objects of my passion. The wilderness was being gobbled up by suburban growth but, when afflicted with sad hours of melancholy brought on by unrequited love, I still sought out a forgotten bit of skunk cabbage swamp or black locust forest in which to walk away my anguish.

Sometimes I carried a knife. It was usually a standard jack-knife with a perennially dull blade. Later, I replaced it with a camper's pocket knife with tiny forks and spoons and cork-screws built in, more of a complicated eating utensil than a weapon. I carried the knife for the sole purpose of carving into a tree my initials along with those of the girl who currently com-manded my affection. These were pre-graffiti days, I suppose, and spray cans and highway abutments were not yet to be considered suitable for public displays of amorous intentions.

It's hard to explain why I preferred carving to confronting the girl of my dreams. I think it was the thrill of holding a knife blade in my hands. My kissing experience was limited, but I must have decided that carving was actually preferable to kissing. A newly perceptible bubble of guilt, however, would sometimes rise in my consciousness. Was I doing permanent damage to the tree? Would it die on my account? I certainly didn't mean any harm to anyone. Like Shakespeare in all those damn sonnets, I wanted to register for immortality sake, my love for . . . let's say . . . Cathy.

I think there were several Cathies back then. Several that I fell in love with, sequentially, that year. Sometimes a name in a song was good enough reason to fall in love. "Cathy's Clown," for example, by the Everly Brothers. I wanted to be Cathy's Clown. And, of course, if I had actually had an audience, I was.

I was hell-bent on a career as a die-hard romantic at this early age of ten or eleven. My major passions in life were: knives, girls, bicycles, and "Leave it to Beaver." The order of priorities would shift from time to time. When things were really bad with my love life, when my knife blade was rusty and when my chain broke on my bike all in the same week, "Leave it to Beaver" would actually command top billing.

There is no way to pinpoint the origin of the carving instinct. Tree after tree in my neighborhood forest was inflicted with the wounds of my adolescent love. Usually it was just a pair of initials circumscribed with the traditional heart. My handiwork was not particularly deep, I don't think, despite the amazing depth of my emotion. Towering willow trees and stalwart oaks were my canvas. Birches seemed too frail and buttonwood trees chipped and fouled my letters. In my world, nothing stayed the same. The universe was in a perpetual state of mutability and decay. Best friends would move away to the suburbs of Washington, D.C. Girls who were one day attracted to me because of my great ability to ride a bicycle without hands would on the morrow forsake me for pug-nose brutes who were incorrigible spellers.

So, as my need for permanence heightened, I sought out the most barrel-chested of beech trees for my work, the statement of love that would endure for a lifetime. Beech trees had shiny gray-silver bark, almost like no bark at all. The carving was hard but the end product was worth it.

By the time I was ready to carve my third Cathy into immortality, I had used up all the lesser beeches and now stalked deeper into the swampy forest to where the most massive of them all stood. Trees closer to the road had been used by other carvers. Some had even undone my handiwork with their own ugly scrawl but this one would be different. I set about my work with diligence.

First a massive heart. The knife was sharp now from recent acquaintance with a file, but the tough rhino hide of the beech tree was a formidable opponent. The pocket-knife blade folded on me twice as I carved, each time slicing neatly across my fingers and causing me to shout in pain. There was no one around to hear but the skunk cabbage. Blood dripped freely, but I carved on, my love for Cathy still strong in my pumping heart.

In the end, the heart looked more like a garlic bulb than the traditional valentine. Then I began to write inside the heart. I had allowed myself room to manipulate. No initials this time. The inscription would read, "Lesley Loves Cathy." I carved the message with elegant, cursory letters to make the emotion more vivid. My wound still smarted but the knife blade now stayed open. At length, the work was complete. I felt like Michelangelo at the Cistine Chapel, DaVinci before "The Last Supper." I folded the bloody knife and put it into my pocket then looked up the tremendous trunk of the grandfather beech. A shaft of late afternoon sunlight found a tunnel through the crowded forest limbs and poured honey-golden light along the spine of the tree. Almost as suddenly, a dark, hungry cloud ate up the sunset and I was plunged into gloom. The throbbing pain in my fingers grew as I began my walk home with the sun fading to gray in the sky over Philadelphia. My walk home would be a harrowing gauntlet of briar vines and smelly swamp plants followed by chastisement from an angry mother whose son had not arrived on time for dinner.

I ran through the briar and brush toward home, feeling every forest ghoul hot on my heels. I was still ringing with pride but worried that I had outdone myself. Then an inexplicable fear swept over me. I had fooled around with mother nature, gone one step too far somehow. I thought I could hear the breathing of other living things close around me as I began to jog and stumble over knotted roots. Footsteps of evil things tramped all around me as I ran for the streetlights and finally arrived at the road and safety.

The next day I rode to Cathy's house to tell her what I had done. I was bolder now. Cathy was playing jump rope in the street with her friends and they all looked puzzled as I arrived. Double Dutch ropes slapped the asphalt with the sound of children being spanked. The ropes stopped. Cathy looked at me. As I tried to apply the foot brakes on my bike, my foot slipped and my pant cuff became caught in the chain. Suicide seemed the only way out now, but I had left my knife at home. The cuff would not be extricated. Worse yet, I realised that I was wearing my old corduroy pants, blue pants with tiny fly-speck points of color scattered down them. The pants that a child would wear. Damn.

Cathy saw my entrapment. "Want some help?" she asked. Her girlfriends snickered.

"Yeah, thanks." Still straddling the bike, I lifted the rear wheel as Cathy bent over and turned the pedal until my pant leg came free.

She stood up and smiled at me. I smiled back. "What are you doing here?" she asked.

"I came to tell you something."

"Oh?" She had a funny look. She knew I was about to say something special and she was trying to get her money's worth.

"I love you," I said. There, it was out.

Just then Cathy's eyes went funny. She wasn't expecting it

outright. She looked at me as if I had just said that tomorrow I would land on the moon.

"Oh," she said.

"I can prove it," I insisted. I meant the tree. What more proof could there be?

"You can?"

"I'll take you there, okay?"

"Okay, when?" I'm sure she had no idea as to what I meant by *there*. How could she? Her other friends had gathered into a huddle and were openly laughing at something. I assumed that I was the subject of the mirth. They could see that I was Cathy's Clown. I didn't care.

"Tomorrow, after school. I'll come get you."

She didn't say yes. She just held onto her funny smile and turned around to her friends who had given up laughing and gone back to jumping rope. Cathy jumped into the midst of the two spinning ropes that were only a blur.

The next day it rained. And the day after that. The third day it was still raining but I went to Cathy's house anyway. Her mother answered the door and said that she wasn't allowed outside, that it was raining and that I was soaking wet. I should go home and change. She asked if I wanted her to phone my mother to come pick me up. I told her it would not be necessary.

I think it rained steadily for the next two weeks. Cathy avoided me at school. No, that's not quite right. She was always surrounded by cronies. There was never an opening to go up and talk to her. She never once broke free of the group to ask me about what I had to show her.

By the time it stopped raining it was too late. Something had changed. I think I still loved her but fate had conspired against me. I had lost whatever courage I once had. I felt cheated and cynical. I couldn't even bring myself to return to the tree.

Five years passed before I arrived back at the giant beech tree. It was a day where I was just out wandering for whatever reasons I had to wander as a teenager into a swampy woods. It was late summer and the air was thick with mosquitoes and gnats. Skunk cabbage blossomed like surreal alien beings all along the floor of the marshy woods. And then, suddenly, I found myself in a clearing of sorts. And there it was.

The names were vivid. The carving had aged well as the bark scarred and then healed. The heart and the names were dark black against the fine silvery beech bark. But something was wrong.

The tree was dead. As I looked up towards its mighty branches, there was not a green leaf to be seen. It had been dead for quite some time. The ground was littered with broken branches and twigs. The sun was streaming down the bareness of the trunk and I stood transfixed in a wash of midday light. I sat down at the base of the tree, my back up against the still sturdy trunk. I guess I wanted to cry.

Pollution could have killed the tree. This last indignant stronghold of wilderness was surrounded by industrial parks and superhighways. Yeah, I told myself, that's what's happened. I hated all of what was transforming the town that I called home. Now it had destroyed something as beautiful and important as this.

But I got up quickly and left the beech tree. I didn't want to study the sacred scars one more time. I shoved aside the briar vines and tramped over the skunk cabbages and walked off home in a sunken cynical rage. I lied to myself for a long time that I was not to blame for any of it.

24

The Pyschology of Nails

O nce every five years I am overcome by an obsessive desire to build something. This usually takes the form of a new addition onto my two hundred-year-old farmhouse.

Because the foundation of the farmhouse is made of loose stone haphazardly piled in a rectangle and since the sills of my house have been providing sustenance for micro-organisms, insects, rodents, reptiles, and assorted small mammals as well as ancestral spirits of varying degrees of dependability — I have never trusted it to support more weight. There's always that chance that I may upset the spiritual vortex that protects the grand old place from total physical dismissal. So I add onto my house by building on but not up.

I add a new piece onto one end or the other. First, I built a small greenhouse which still displays all the mistakes possible for a first-time builder. Second, a north-end addition of two storeys that, out of caution, was so overbuilt, that I could park tandem trailer trucks on the roof, and finally this summer's project.

The time had come for me to build an addition onto the addition. It runs east toward the sunrise, fit snugly against an old wall which will never see the sun again. The nomenclature of geometry lacks any single word that indicates the actual shape of the new structure but it exists in a multi-tiered sort of fashion conforming to the shape of the land beneath it.

Think of my house if you will as a living thing that grows a new, sometimes giant, appendage every few years. I am the eternal organism, symbiotically relating to my house, that says, almost biologically, yes, the time has come. We need a new arm, a new leg, or another brain. So the house blossoms an addition through the summer. Footings are poured, foundations erected (well concrete pillars at least), and walls appear.

Mine has become one of those New Englandish houses that looks like it is wandering off somewhere. Often there is a barn to link up with at the other end of the line. All that's left of my barn, however, is a forlorn square fence of lichen-varnished rocks. So my house will have to settle for its journey into the wilderness, slow but sure.

My old house was built upon an island of actual soil and stone wedged between a bedrock hillside and a fertile, though incontinent bog. The first addition came perilously close to the bog, and I had to cease growing there to the north. Instead, I decided to tack east away from the north bog and confront the bedrock head on. Now I could have opted for dynamite and rock drilling or maybe just a very ambitious bulldozer but I hated the idea. I remembered one thing from Sunday School —- that it was okay to build your house upon a rock, so I decided to hell with digging deep, pouring footings, and building foundation walls, for my new addition would already be tilting up the hill like an Everest mountaineer. Instead, I'd rip into the bedrock a bit, pour some boxed footings, then settle for twelve-inch concrete posts.

That's when the fun started. I rented my first jackhammer. Up until that moment of vibratory ecstasy I had been a jack-hammer virgin. The man at the U-rent lined me up with a Kango Hammer. Just set her on the rock, hang on, and let her rip.

I spent my Easter weekend, as it turned out, banging away at the bedrock. I grew weary at length and hired a local teen-ager to come give me some help. At first he was cautious but soon he looked like someone who had found the meaning of life. Maybe it was his first honest employment. Or maybe it was the fact that the Kango sounded a lot like Def Leopard played backwards at full volume. Whatever it was, I allowed my blisters to cool, my back to recover, and I paid Gary to continue to chew slate long after I was ready to retreat to iced tea for the summer.

We slopped in some concrete for footings in the right places and then propped up those round cardboard tubes to pour posts. Now if you can keep dry cement from blowing into your eyes, and if you don't mind hauling endless wheelbarrows of wet gray gunk, concrete work is not bad. A little water, a little sand, a little Portland Cement, and — *Voila!* Once you've pour-ed it into the tubes, it's a bit like baking a cake. I'll avoid the fine points of it, but never forget to tamp it down with the butt-end of a 2 x 4 to get out all the air. Then hope it doesn't rain.

My big problem with construction is that I can never get anything exactly square. I followed a book this time that explained how to do it with string and corner boards (batter boards they're called — like in cake baking again). Well, shoot. My concrete posts weren't in exactly the right spot. My structure had unwittingly gone trapezoidal on me. Only slightly. But it would mean endless minor revisions later. Tuck in a wall here, push out a wall slightly there.

Realizing my first primal error — six inches or so off, — I forged onward. I placed my wooden beams on the concrete posts. Hell, they looked square. I leveled them as much as a human could expect to level anything and I pushed onward.

I find that building is a manic depressive activity for me. One minute I'm confident as Goliath that I can do anything with a hammer, a saw, a couple of nails, and maybe a piece of wood or two. Next, I discover that I am a hopeless buffoon among building materials, that I can't possibly create a pigeon coop let alone a structure for human occupation. So I ride the wave up and down as the building progresses or stagnates, as the case may be. I usually work alone so no one sees the emotional roller coaster.

In fact, to digress, it takes a monumental amount of courage to begin a largish structure of any sort. Since I am completely lacking in such courage, I have to depend almost entirely on the foolhardiness and blind optimism that have served me so well during these thirty-eight years. While these two are not advisable substitutes for courage, skill or building knowledge, I often have to make do.

This will not be an absolute and precise picture of the whole construction, I promise you. If it were, it would become as tedious as your uncle's slides of Pensecola. And I need to spare you some of the heartbreak of such things as anchor bolts that refuse to set properly in concrete, saw blades that go dull and the like.

So, assume that I've argued my way with physics and geometry past the fact that my corners will not be perfectly square or my sills one hundred percent level. Once you put in the joists and the rough flooring, a magical thing happens: you have a flat, more or less regular surface upon which to build. The miracle: you frame a wall. If that was all there was to building, I'd have my entire acreage under construction. It's just so much damn fun. Bang a few boards together (2 x 6s in my case), and prop it up into place. Suddenly you've framed in the sky. The next wall is even easier because you have a first wall to set up against. When you get to the fourth wall, you pray it won't be too snug or too loose. And if it is, you bash one wall or the other into place with a sledge hammer. Never underestimate the value of a good sledge hammer when wood won't do exactly what you want it to do.

But mysteries abound in building. Suppose you're cutting a whole bunch of studs to, say, 96 inches. Everything is going fine until suddenly you've lost a quarter inch somewhere. It begins as an innocent eighth inch . . . which you don't notice. But next thing you know, that quarter inch crops up. Next it's a 5/16 of an inch. Suddenly all hell brakes loose. You mismeasure and you're an inch or two short. Cursing under the open skies. Recovery means re-cutting or tearing out a few boards.

Lost things are the bane of the amateur builder. Tape measures have vanished without a trace . . . never to surface again. Hammers wander off for a lunch break in the woods. Memorized dimensions sometimes convolute and shift at random in the cluttered warehouse of the mind. But worst of all are pencils. You can't build without pencils but pencils do not a worksite love. At most any worksite, ask six good carpenters and the best you'll come up with is one inch-and-a-half stub of a blunt end pencil. Pencils have wings. They are as alive as anything growing in the dankness of my basement or anything that flies above my marsh.

I started my building project with a set of twenty-four healthy new, Eberhard Number 2, soft yellow pencils liberated from the English Department exclusively for this project. Within hours, my stock was reduced to twelve, within days I was down to three, and by the end of the week I had one short stub of pencil that my life depended upon. I'd sharpened it meticulously with a knife lest I lose its length altogether and be left with nothing but an eraser.

Then arrives the dreaded moment when that pencil too has disappeared. There are no others in the house and pens are not to be trusted. So one searches high and low, rants and raves, accuses the family of theft, and denounces dead relatives. The entire universe has conspired against the builder. You quit for coffee, in desperation, not wanting to go on building at all. Suddenly, there it is; it was perched above your ear all the time. Pencils are like that.

Nails, though are something else. I've worked with many kinds of nails — common nails, galvanized nails, ringed nails, diamond tipped nails (the shape that is), round head nails, and more. There is a psychology to nails that I have only begun to learn. When moulded from molten steel, nails harden with magnificent personalities, each different from the rest, each with a will of its own.

The first time you learn this is when you carry a fifty pound box of five penny (5D) nails across the yard. It transmutes gravity in such a way that it seems more like a hundred. The cardboard box is welded shut with staples and glue. It takes a crowbar to get the box open. But then suddenly, there you are, staring at an open box of pristine blue-gray five penny common nails. It's a beautiful sight to behold. They look so easy to work with. So trusting.

So you choose your favorite hammer and go to work. Then the lessons begin. A nail loves a knot in wood like no other thing on the face of the earth. No matter how hard you try, a nail will seek out and imbed itself in the nearest knot available as you build. You bash away believing that steel is harder than wood only to see the nail curl like a worm and lie down to die beside the flat of the board only to be irretrievably stuck in what little of the knot it penetrated. It's like a salmon going upstream to spawn and then die.

Sledge hammers are of no avail. Claw hammers sometimes work but often a crow bar is the only way out. I've tried living without a two foot crow bar before and found life intolerable. Take my advice and always have one lingering nearby, ready for use.

A nail too, I've discovered, likes to seek out and do battle with other nails. Maybe the ones I buy are made of lodestone, I don't know. If possible, a nail driven into the sheathing of a wall will seek out the head of another nail, sending a ringing, bone-chilling tremor down the arm of the hammerer.

Modern building materials have aided the nail, giving it the ability to fly as well. You see, once you have your framed wall up, you probably will want to sheath it with something before the siding. Sheathing is like a first wall. You can use boards or plywood or (what I use) waferboard. This new unglamorous material is made from wood chips compressed and glued together. It is insidious stuff but the price is right. The problem is with the nailing. Somehow the surface of waferboard is hard to penetrate. A nail, once struck, will cause a mighty bounce if not careful. It takes a long while to get the hang of making a nail stick to waferboard. You position the nail carefully over the stud, you swing, you make contact, then suddenly your nail has joined the space program. Documented by videotape, I have, on several occasions, launched nails in earth orbit. Lunar probes are next.

The only way I've found to make nails stay put or avoid knots and other nails is this: I sneak up on them. This is the ultimate psychology of nails. The more concentrated attention you give a nail, the more it will want to launch into the ozone or twist like a South Philadelphia soft pretzel. So, instead, I pretend I'm not interested. I casually hold the nail between thumb and forefinger, pull back on the hammer and then look the other way. I let the nail know that I don't give a damn. Then let fly. It usually works.

When, however, the psychology backfires, one must be ready to pay the price of smashed thumb and fingers. I wore black and blue thumbs this past summer like small dark emblems of my battles with nails. Blood blisters bloomed as well at finger tips where an erudite hammer had found flesh instead of steel. I've grown to accept the abuse as part of building. One small consolation is that a smashed thumb grants license to the smashee for one loud whoop of pain. My rural neighbors have now grown accustomed to my outbursts through the warmer months. I find that a very loud yell is essential. Whimpering does no good, muffled cries of anguish are of little use at all, but a good strong, involuntary howl diminishes the pain almost immediately. I've cultivated a strong, impregnable yelp as well that can punctuate the stillness for at least a mile. And I always feel okay afterwards, ready to go on, realizing again that pain is just part of a builder's life like sawdust and lost pencils.

Building, of course, is not all masochism. After the spasms of pain and the moments of discontent over a warped stud or inaccurate lintel comes the gloating. Like other builders, I suspect, I like to congratulate myself over my accomplishments. A two story building is, after all, more satisfying to look at than just a whole bunch of words on a typed page. So at the end of most days I like to gloat. I tell myself what a damn fine job I've done. (I only do this in private . . . I don't gloat among humans, just nails and wood.)

Then, nearing the brink of autumn, I realize that I've done it. I've sealed in the shell of the house. There are windows fit into the holes left in the walls, shingles are fit snug over the roof sheathing. Doors are aligned. A crazy assortment of building materials has coalesced to become one with the old house. The first rain from the southeast drives rivers of water into the new structure, so more caulking ensues. Aside from a few days of help from loyal and trusted friends, the whole darn thing was made with just my own hands. Self-congratulations all around long into the night.

But then, a moment of truce. The building inspector arrives. He tells me he has a bad back and doesn't want to climb around too much. I commiserate. But I also realize the man has the right to tell me my addition is a shambles. I should tear it down and forget it. I lead him gingerly about the place. He studies my studs, fingers the door jambs, wonders out loud about proper ventilation for the insulation. Then we are on the second floor and he is studying the roof joists.

"Not much pitch to it," he says, meaning the slope of the roof. "You could got a lot of weight up there. Wet snow."

"I expect the wind will blow it off," I counter.

"Probably, but you never know. I'm wondering if that meets with the Code."

God, not the *Code*. He means the building code, of course. Something I'm not at all familiar with. But alas, this is Nova

Scotia, not New Jersey. His tone is tempered. He wonders instead of orders. In other parts of the world, I would get arrested for these structural worries. Here, it's just a cause of wonderment.

"Yep, I think that this roof might not have quite as much support as it wants."

"Do you think this is a major problem?" I ask, swallowing my chewing gum.

"Not necessarily," he says. "Only thing that could happen is that the roof might fall down on you at some point." I almost expect him to say, "Aside from that, I wouldn't worry." Instead he says that he's got to go.

"I'll brace them better . . . the joists I mean. That should do it."

"It might," he says and climbs down the ladder to leave. "You wouldn't want it to sag. You know what it's like to drive down the road and see a sagging roof."

"Yeah, I see what you mean." In my mind's eye I see my ruler edged ridgepole all slouching under a ton of heavy wet snow. The inspector had been kind. I'll brace like hell, I promise — cross braces, floor supports. He's been gentle with me and damn if I won't fix up the roof to be ready for the next ice age.

But before the summer quietly dies I have one more encounter with the authorities. For up to the time of the building inspector I had operated in a social vacuum, my only contact with the outside world that of phone orders to the building supply and small talk with the delivery men. But now, even as I finish with a final caulking, lo and behold, the tax assessor.

"You're a bit early aren't you? I'm not even done yet."

"Oh, that's okay. I wanted to drive out here by the beach anyway." The city was hot, he was looking for an out-of-town excuse.

"What's under your old house anyway?" he asks looking at some paperwork on his clipboard.

"Loose stone foundation and a dirt floor."

"Son of a gun, we have you down here for a full basement."

"What about that part of your house?" He means my first addition.

"It has concrete but just a crawl space. Take a look." He does.

"Jeez, we had that wrong too."

"And I'd say the dimensions of this addition aren't what we had on file. It's a bit smaller. What do you know?"

I stay out of his way, high up on the ladder. He wanders and examines and prods and measures only to return to tell me that his records are all wrong.

"You've been paying too much on this, you know. We're going to have to adjust your records."

I pay about two hundred dollars a year in property tax. When I tell this to my American friends, they can't believe it. Now I learn I've been paying too much.

"I don't know if we can get you a refund, but we'll try. Meanwhile, I'll get this file corrected. Good luck with the building. Gosh it's nice to be out of the city."

"Thanks."

The tax assessor leaves. My caulking gun is drooling a long brown dollop of acrylic redwood mucous down my leg. I size up the world again. Yep, this is the way it works in Nova Scotia. The tax assessor comes out to size up the estate. He finds five good reasons to lower my taxes, then drives off. I might get a refund I think. Can I collect backwards the full two hundred years of the house? Will they pay me for the interest on the overpayment? I expect letters of apologies, a cheque for the grievous error.

Maybe I don't understand the ways of the world after all. Maybe something weird has happened while I worked away with my boards and hammer all summer. I back off the pressure on the caulking gun and try to wipe the caulking off my pants only to find my hand glued to my leg. I hobble down the ladder, hand stuck to thigh, and look again at my building. The real world will catch up with me soon enough. Right now dreams and hard physical truth are all the same. That's what building is all about anyway.

You take a piece of rock and build something on it. Then you build a wall and frame in the field, then a roof and frame in the sky. Then the sadness of closing in the walls, covering it all up. Then a nice guy with a bad back tells how to fix a few worries so it won't fall down and he sends after him a fellow with a clipboard to lower your taxes to ease the load on your pocketbook. And then you stand there in the late summer slant of sun, one half of your body caulked into paralysis, and try to figure it all out. There's a sweet feeling inside, like you just found a new truth that you can use to sheathe in all the happiness of your family, like you just figured out why you're alive and dreaming and building your life away in Nova Scotia.

25

On Strike

B eing on strike hasn't been one of the most exciting experiences of my life. I went on strike partly because I had never gone on strike before but now that I was two weeks into it, I decided I would rather get on with more important things.

At this point in the game, the strike was about the most obvious and mundane of worries: money. The schematics of our grievances were rather complex and boring and I won't trouble you but the bottom line was that most of us didn't feel that we were being paid well enough for the work we did. Even though I was walking up and down Coburg Road with a strike placard, I confess that my heart was not in it. You see, the truth is that teaching in a university is downright fun. I know I'll catch hell for saying it. But it isn't like real work at all.

When I'm not on strike, I am employed by the government to talk to intelligent, inquisitive young adults about literature, the imagination, writing, and so forth. I hold discussions concerning novels and poetry and we debate ideas. In truth, I would probably be doing these things if anyone was paying me or not. Don't get me wrong; I take my job seriously and I put a lot of energy into it. It's just that it doesn't feel like work.

In fact, I think I started teaching at university because I was having a hard time finding enough interesting and intelligent people out there in the real world to banter with. I was getting tired of discussing radial tires, the price of a cord of firewood, and who was high sticking in hockey. This is important stuff, I know, but my mind was beginning to turn into a beer commercial. So I went looking for a way to discuss the mutability of time, Jungian dream analysis, the special theory of relativity, and some of my favorite books. Much to my surprise it turned out that colleges and universities were good places for this sort of exchange.

At first it was just a matter of hanging around the cafeterias and striking up a conversation. The trouble was that too many students were all caught up in doing homework and readings for their courses. I had played that game too for so many years that I didn't think I should get back on the wheel again. Besides, I had a couple of degrees that I figured I should put to work. Just maybe, I thought, they might let me teach.

Sure enough, somebody thought I was fit for teaching. It sounded like great fun. I thought it would be a great avenue for getting all those ideas out of my head and into the minds of my students. Then came the kicker. I was told by the English Department chairperson that somebody would even pay me for it. I suggested that it wasn't necessary, but I retracted that statement immediately, noticing that it brought a sour grimace of mistrust in the face of my new boss.

Over the years the pay kept creeping up until I had an income above the poverty line. I began buying things to fill up my house. I ate more food and wasted more money. It grew slightly depressing. Then the university started giving me more money each year for doing the same damn job. This was quite a complement but it seemed completely absurd.

I really wanted to yell and scream. I wanted to say that I was overpaid, that I liked my job, it was a privilege meeting and talking with these young, intelligent, polite kids. I wanted to explain that all the money was making me into a slob. But I kept my mouth shut. If I so much as peeped that I was unhappy with my continual raises, I knew I'd be fired, possibly sent to the provincial mental hospital. I grumbled among my colleagues. I wanted to know the logic of the system.

One colleague explained to me that the theory was this. The more years that I taught the more qualified I became, and therefore the more worthy of a higher salary. I was, ipso facto, a better teacher because I had more time to practice and accumulate more knowledge.

I disagreed passionately. I still loved teaching, I explained, but I knew for a fact that I wasn't quite as energetic, enthusiastic, and dynamic as I was when I started out at twenty years of age. I had been teaching for fifteen years. My energy level just wasn't as high. I put on a good show, but I just couldn't sprint my intellect the way I could when I was newly wedded to academia. I should be paid less. The poor starving young kids fresh out of graduate school with minds finely tuned liked immaculate harpsichord strings should be paid more than me.

My colleagues couldn't quite see my point.

Then it occurred to me that maybe *I* should go on strike . . . all by myself. I would demand lower wages. I chewed on it long and hard but my wife talked me out of it. Everyone would call me a lunatic. The entire population of North America would be angry at me. I would probably be arrested. But worse yet . . . no one would ever listen to me seriously or enter into a significant intellectual dialogue ever again with me.

I had no choice. I kept my mouth shut.

Then came 1988 and the strike at Dalhousie University. The issues were complex and disagreeable but it boiled down to money. Lack of money meant lack of respect. We weren't being paid what we deserved. My union had been befuddled by the university for a few years over wage fairness. (I think the words that often cropped up were "equity" and "parity.") Cynicism had soured the fruit of knowledge. Almost everyone but me wanted to walk out so I simply decided that the great minds surrounding me knew more than I did for these were not matters that commanded my attention.

I went on strike because I wanted to see my fellow teachers happier. I like seeing people happy, especially academics who have a harder time at happiness than most because of all that intellectual brooding which continually goes on in their heads. I wanted to be loyal to my compatriots. I wanted a strong, short strike so we would all go back to our classrooms with smile buttons.

Also there was this: I had never been on strike before. It was early fall. The weather was good. Maybe it would be fun to walk up and down a Halifax city street with other intellectuals. Maybe I'd make some new friends, share some radical ideas. So I was compelled beyond reason to go on strike. Besides, I needed that experience for my experience rack. At thirty-seven I had used up most of my fantasies. I had surfed the big waves on the North Shore of Oahu in winter; I had written books; I had made love to a beautiful woman on the grounds of the Washington Monument. And I was getting too old for real danger. So I would do this. I would give up my strike virginity and see what happened.

The first day was great. My buddies were ebullient. After an hour and a half, I agreed with a Classics instructor, that yes, gol darn it, walking was good for your breathing and for your spirit. It was better than being stuffed up in an office correcting dangling modifier problems in essays. We carried signs that said the usual things. The university, it seemed, had shackled us to a life of poverty and overwork.

I liked carrying the sign that said, "Building a Better University. Sorry for the Inconvenience." I learned how to make the placard tack against the wind when powerful gusts whipped up from the city buses. I smiled at all the passersby and always moved out of their way. I tried to learn more about the issues from other walkers but it all boiled down to the same old stuff. There were evil men up in the administration stuffing their shirts with the money we deserved. They were conspiring at this very minute to fire us all and hire a hundred or so unemployed academics from Pakistan who would work for much less.

I kept wondering why my friends and colleagues were so dedicated to this cause when much bigger problems existed in the world. Why weren't they out marching to get rid of nuclear missiles or acid rain or toxic waste or racial hatred? Why were they (why was I!) out marching for a couple of extra dollars that would primarily be emptied from out of our pockets by taxes anyway?

We had a point to prove, I was reminded, and we weren't going to be kicked around.

On TV we looked like selfish beggars. Our adversaries made it sound like they had already done backflips to meet our demands but that we were stubborn sons and daughters of bitches who would not be budged. Our greed, it appeared, was indefatigable.

Where was truth? I wondered. Nowhere to be found. I canvassed other walkers of the line. One was an immigrant from Hungary who taught chemistry in the Pharmacy Department. The last time she had walked the streets carrying a sign was during the revolution in Hungary in 1956. Russian tanks had rolled into Budapest then to put an end to the complainers. "This must seem ludicrous compared to 1956," I said.

"It's different but sort of the same," was all she said. I had a hard time seeing the parallel.

I remembered previous times I had walked the streets for a cause. Most recently, it had been to remove nuclear missiles from Halifax Harbour where they vacationed periodically in American submarines. Another time I had demonstrated at Province House to ban the herbicide spraying of deadly chemicals 2–4–D and 2–4–5–T. And going way back, there had been the march in downtown New York to protest the bombing of Cambodia, and before that, massive gatherings of angry protesters in Washington to protest other atrocities of the

Vietnam War. Now I was marching for a new VCR and a compact disc player. I was steam-rolling on an odyssey away from the green pastures of the lunatic fringe toward the center ground of materialism and financial well-being.

After a few days, the discussions on the front line grew more animated with hostility toward the reportedly corrupt university administration. The president of the university was reported to have redecorated his house this year for two hundred thousand dollars. This included a hot tub, the report suggested. His wife, as well, had been endowed by the university with an enormous budget for social occasions. (Did they use the hot tub, I queried, at formal academic banquets?)

Then there was the problem of the few faculty who had not gone on strike. These were scurrilous, disloyal traitors. Clearly, these were academics without backbone or any stitch of moral fortitude. And to think that they would profit from our protests once this was over and we all had our salaries hiked.

Letters had poured in, the union reported, from university faculties all over Canada — Concordia, St. Mary's, Manitoba and the University of Victoria. We were in their hearts and minds. We were on the vanguard of something important. "This is just the tip of the iceberg," someone from Anatomy said to me. "Soon they'll be marching all over Canada against underfunding of universities."

There was a sense of grandness and wonder here. Why was I not feeling a chill up my spine? I think it was because I felt like a fraud. I wanted to shout it out: "Where were you when the nuclear-armed subs entered Halifax Harbour and I failed to muster enough support to blockade the harbour mouth with sail boats, zodiacs, wind surfers and kayaks?" But I didn't say a thing.

I quietly pledged that I would give away any profit from this endeavor to the Adopt-a-Grandmother Foundation. I had read the brochure carefully. There was a homeless, blind, one-armed woman in Peru who I could feed and clothe for less than a dollar a day. Maybe I was on strike for her. Or so I counseled myself.

Only recently had I heard from another charity that I had patronized. My twenty bucks had gone to buy an ox (or at least part of that ox) for a mother of three in Mali, Africa, one of the poorest nations on earth. Maybe I could buy somebody else an entire ox with the proceeds from this strike. And yes, maybe we should march to the president's house, rip out the hot tub, even as the vice-presidents and their handmaidens lounged and bubbled. Yes, indeed, rip it out, plumbing and all, sell it to the highest bidder and buy food for an entire Ethiopian village for a year.

On the tenth day, ice pellets began to fall from the sky. As I continued to walk the line, a friend from the English Department told me about a meat packing plant in his hometown of Brooks, Alberta. The men had gone on strike there and the strike lasted three years. Workers camped out and marched day in and day out for three years, surviving the freezing blasts of the arctic. They were local heroes. Of sorts. But nothing came of the strike. Scabs were hired and the meat packers never made it back to work. Hmm.

Canada is no place to walk the picket line in the winter. It's why the post office workers always go on strike in the summer. Our strike would be brief, I hoped.

I began to long for a warm, academically comfortable classroom. There were no new ideas on the picket line. We were good guys, they were bad. I couldn't get a new filing cabinet for my office but the vice president for academic affairs had his office refurbished.

Looking back on the strike in my ever-pragmatic sort of mind, I see that the highlight was not so much the dialogue but the car that would pull up at least once every hour with fresh coffee and Tim Horton donuts. Tim Horton was making a staggering profit from our strike. But I was becoming a connoisseur of Dutchies, double glazed, and chocolate-coconut donuts. I watched my colleagues, nearly as gluttonous as I was.

The talk was almost exclusively about the strike and the quality of the provisions provided from our union strike fund. We had become obsessed with wages and donuts. The rest of the intellectual world had been whittled away.

I grew tired of the diatribes and sometimes wandered off down a side street, still carrying my sign: "Building a Better University." I began to think about the strike pay, now up to two hundred dollars a week. Since my job was half-time, I was making about the same wage as when I was actively teaching my six classes a week. Now, the hours were fewer. What if I went uptown, I wondered and walked into the Derby Tavern? What if I said, "Gather round, sad drinkers, I have an offer? Who would like to walk up and down Coburg Road for an hour and a half at a time, four times a week, free coffee and donuts until you bust and we'll pay you two hundred smackers a week? Who wants the job?"

My guess is that there'd be one empty tavern up there. And at that point, with my mercenary strikers at work holding signs and gulping donuts, I'd be morally free to pursue other activities. Then maybe I'd call up a few of my students and invite them by for a beer. I'd spend what was left of my hard-earned strike pay on them just to strike up a few good conversations about negative capability, the *carpe diem* motif or Nietzsche's view of God. Or maybe I'd just explain why I think that garbage men and oil rig workers deserve big bucks for their hard labor and why professors should live a bit more like peasants . . . maybe not all the time, but, say, one year out of three.

But the sad truth is that I would tough it out with my colleagues simply out of mock loyalty. I longed to be back in the classroom and away from the diesel fumes, ice pellets, and manicheistic unionism. I rationalized that I should stick it out until the end, come hell or high water, in hopes that next time, when the world is about to end and I need a few comrades to take to the streets, I'll knock upon the doors of academe and my own worries won't fall on deaf ears.

26
Love and the Loading Bay

I've spent only a small part of my life working at jobs that required hard physical labor. Usually money is just a happy accident for me, but there was a time when I was paying my way through college and was desperate for the highest hourly wage my physical body could stand.

I didn't look like I was cut out to load trucks, but I got the job at North Penn Transfer because my father worked there as a mechanic. Since I could expect to get union wages as an irregular Teamster, it would probably be the most money I'd see for the next decade or so. The only real problem with the job, however, was that I had to work graveyard shift, ten at night to seven in the morning.

Little did I know that I was about to enter into a nocturnal nightmare of an occupation. I mean, I really didn't mind the lugging of the world's freight from trailer to trailer along the loading floor. It was the readjustment of my biological clock that made for problems.

First night on the job, the dispatcher told me next to nothing about the work. He gave me a clipboard of shipping bills and teamed me up with guy named Mario. Mario was maybe two hundred pounds heavier than me and had actually spent some time in a Philadelphia Eagles training camp before the serious cuts were made. When the partnerships were set up, I guess Mario felt cheated, getting stuck with a tall, skinny, long-haired hippie like myself. I swore I'd do my best as a freight jockey and I still believe I didn't do half bad. Mario stopped poking fun of me by the second night and we got along okay.

Clarence was the dispatcher. Sometimes he was called Black Clarence because there was a White Clarence who was mostly seen only in the daytime, White Clarence being the boss. However, he wasn't the *Big Boss* since that was another man who lived somewhere in Pennsylvania and never showed his face here in Jersey.

Night-time Clarence was a recently retired army sergeant from Fort Dix. I didn't like the looks of that. He shouted a lot even when he wasn't angry and, oh boy, look out if you screwed up. I screwed up a few times on my first week and nobody seemed surprised. I think I shipped off twelve cases of toilet paper that should have gone to a restaurant in Atlantic City to a computer company in Secaucus. Maybe I did stuff worse than that, I don't know.

The novelty of the job kept me going strong until about three hours into it on the first night. Then I discovered I was dead tired, ready to fall involuntarily asleep. It was way past my bed time. What little adrenalin that had kept me chugging at the start had been siphoned off somewhere. It was one o'clock in the morning and I was ready to conk out. Suddenly it occurred to me that this whole fiasco must have been some extraordinary joke. I felt so tired and so bad that I realized people couldn't possibly spend their nights living through this hell. It had to be some magnificent hoax. It had to be. There was no way I could keep on loading boxes of cleaning agents, engine parts and roofing shingles until seven o'clock in the morning.

Mario was off in search of a hard-to-find shipment of PVC pipe. I looked around for some sympathy and saw one other frail human replica of total fatigue. I think his name was Donald but he was known on the loading bay as No Doz. No Doz was a lanky, blond-haired guy about my own age who seemed to have discovered the secret of keeping your body in motion while your mind was totally asleep.

"It's a goof, right?" I asked him. "I mean, nobody stays awake all night."

"You're right," he answered as if in a dream. "You get to sleep during lunch."

"Lunch?"

"Yeah, one more hour."

Lunch. At two o'clock in the morning. The joke grew darker as the night stars blossomed unseen above the roof of the loading dock. I tried to keep my mind on my work, thinking that somehow *lunch* would be a blissful hour of respite. I repeated the word over and over in my head as working men and women down through the centuries had done before me, focusing on something hopeful, something to allow you out of the agonizing nightmare of employment: lunch.

Two o'clock rolled around. Hand trucks rolled to a stop and the men filed into the lunch room, a windowless cubicle, nine feet by nine feet. There were three vandalized vinyl love seats — double chairs big enough for two people. Bodies slumped down into them and began to eat Wonder Bread sandwiches of bologna or tuna fish. There was no place for me to sit except the dirty linoleum floor. I sat.

The conversation was about different people and how fucked up they were. I didn't know any of the subjects under discussion but everyone else did and they all agreed that every soul named was a fuck-up. I wanted to ask if they were former employees or what. Was that why they all knew these fuck-ups? Or was it something else? Was there a local bar where every-one went on Saturday night to meet fucked-up men and women just so there would be something to talk about during lunch?

I was afraid to ask. I was too tired to move my jaws so I just allowed myself to drift off into a hazy nowhere. Maybe while I slept, they talked about me. I'll never know. But I do remember my dream. In my dream I was simply home, asleep in bed, dreaming that I had acquired a night job loading trucks.

Nobody woke me up when lunch was over. When the sound of a flushing toilet woke me, I looked at the clock: 3:15. I was overextending my lunch. Shoot. I got up, shook the dust off my pants and the sleep out of my foggy, rattled brain.

Everybody got a good laugh out of me stumbling out of the break room. Clarence gave me moderate hell and I apologized. I decided that it didn't matter much anyway because it all had to be a bad joke or a lousy pepperoni pizza dream.

I cornered No Doz again and, this time, asked him about his nick name. He said, sure, he had tried the pills but that they made him run to the bathroom every fifteen minutes. "I guess that's how they keep you awake," he said. He had no other pearls of wisdom as to how to stay awake. "I guess you just get used to it," he said, his eyes curtained down to a thin visual field of possibility.

Miraculously, I survived the first night. It was an enlightening experience. I learned something new about the relativity of time. I discovered that the hours of the day between four a.m. and seven a.m. expand exponentially with the weariness of the observer. I ceased to believe that the sun would ever come up again, that the world would ever turn back to daylight. All around me zombies pushed their handtrucks. My senses became overly tuned into every sound, every smell. It was a hell of propane forklift exhaust, top forty music from a raspy broken down transistor radio and other nauseating nuances. Mario tried to cheer me up with a pat on the back now and then but I failed to respond. It wasn't until I was trying to lift a two hundred gallon barrel of industrial poison and my hand truck pinned me to the wall that Mario broke me out of my miasma. I went from exhausted, irreversible boredom to sheer terror in the course of a few seconds. The hand truck handle was driven into my spleen and I could hardly breathe. Good old Mario lifted the massive barrel with his arms and freed me from my prison, then slapped me on the back and explained how you have to "break" the lift of something as heavy as that. To break a barrel or a heavy load, you have to kick out the bottom wheels with your foot and push down, not out with your arms. "Got it," I said.

I looked around. Naturally, I had a full audience. It was the moment they had all been waiting for.

The moment of terror at least had brought me back to the land of the living. I was now fully awake. Mario offered to get the other eleven barrels of poison but I declined to let him. It was one of those moments when a man was tested. I cracked one then another off the floor. Rolling them with a semblance of control and then tooling them up a ramp into the back of a forty-foot trailer was another matter. I conjured various spiritual forces for assistance and, at length, discovered that I had loaded the ass-end of a tractor trailer with an even dozen green, oversize steel barrels marked in bold skull and cross bones POISON in little less than a half an hour. I figured the net weight of the chemicals alone was over one hundred times my own weight in toxic merchandise. It was one of the prouder moments in the history of my labor.

Within minutes, I detected a rosy glow coming from an empty bay door. I immediately assumed that lugging all those chemicals had swamped my brain and I was hallucinating. I asked No Doz if he saw it too.

"I don't see anything," he said, his eyelids nearly fused shut. No wonder he couldn't see anything. No Doz had given up on caffeine pills and had perfected somnambulism as a means of surviving the job.

I discovered that dawn brought a spurt of new energy, like

a small flare shot up briefly into the sky. I moved on to loading seventy five cartons of florescent light bulbs destined for a diner in Perth Amboy. It was apparent from the sound of the contents that the lights had long since turned to shredded glass. Fearful that I might get blamed for the damage, I drew Mario aside and shook a carton in his face. The glass fragments crashed around inside with the sound of a car tire driving over the winter's first frozen puddle.

"What's the problem?" Mario asked.

"They're all busted. What do I do?"

"Nothing. Just load 'em. Here. Like this." He picked the carton out of my hand and, holding it like an Olympic javelin, he sent it sailing twenty feet forward into the trailer.

Unfortunately, Clarence was right behind us.

"Problem, boys?"

"Nuthin'," Mario said.

I couldn't keep my mouth shut. "They're all busted anyway," I said.

Clarence grimaced. "I didn't hear that. Load 'em up anyway and send 'em on. If we know they're all busted, I got a pile of papers I have to fill out and I hate nothing more than filling out forms."

Clarence picked up a carton of fragmented light tubes and shook it so the glass smashed around inside. "Nothing wrong with these lights."

"Not a thing," said Mario. So I loaded up the lot of them and went on to the next job.

The theory was this: I'd go home, eat breakfast and go to sleep. Wake up at four o'clock in the afternoon, eat supper, then go see my girlfriend and be back at work by ten, raring to go.

But curiously enough, sleep had given up hope. It was tired of waiting around for me to get home and had moved on to other parts of the world by nine o'clock in the morning. I couldn't fall asleep. I tossed and turned for hours, then fell into a fitful stupor, only to be awakened by my mom late in the afternoon and told that supper was ready.

I ate like a zombie and, afterwards, hopped in my car to pick up my girlfriend. We went some place deep in the woods to make out for a few hours, then the evil time rolled around when I would have to be back at work. I drove her back home, cursing my new occupation but milking it for all the sympathy it was worth. I kissed her goodnight and drove off in darkness towards North Penn.

This was a screwball universe, I decided, as I re-established my relationship with the handtruck I had used the night before. Somebody had painted names on all the handtrucks. Mine had been graced with the name "Gladys." Gladys and I would spend the night together.

I was pretty much a novice at shoptalk in those days, but I was surrounded by men of great practiced rhetoric. Like all scholars, they were specialized, limited in discursive range, but the subjects were of universal application and interest. After my first night on the job, I thought it would all be lectures and dialogue on people who were fuck-ups and how fucked-up the world was. The job was fucked-up, for example. We all knew that. The hours were plain screwed.

Taxes, naturally, were fucked-up. I hadn't seen my first pay check but, according to the guys, the union dues, the unemployment insurance, and the state and federal taxes were going to feast fully on it before it found its way to me.

On and on ran the list of how fouled-up the world was. Problems with weather, pollution, traffic, traffic cops, car engines, prices of seat covers, ticks, television shows that were canceled. I tried to join in the conversation but I just didn't have the understanding, the all-embracing grudge against the world that fueled the dialogue of my fellow workers. Each time I tried to explain that I too was bummed-out about something — they'd fail to see my point.

"Why the hell do we need money, anyway?" I'd ask Mario or No Doz. "Heck, I mean, nobody really needs much to live on. All you do with money is buy stuff, mostly things you don't need, right?"

It seemed to me I was onto something. Nobody liked their job. So why not learn to just get by without money. I was willing to move out into the woods, for example, and build my own house out of trees and forget about work and earning money just to buy garbage.

The boys just couldn't see my point. I had made the fatal flaw of going beyond pure, hard cynicism into the realm of solution. Foolish, naive, yes, but we were just bullshitting, right? Just trying to kill time. I wanted *in* on the action.

Eddie, the Greek guy who ran the forklift, was walking from the john when he heard my little diatribe. He stopped in his tracks, still zipping up his fly, took a hard right hand turn, walked up to me until I could smell the olive oil and feta cheese on his breath. He was pissed-off at the world as always but now he had found someone beneath him in seniority to get pissed-off at: me.

"What the fuck you think we are, a bunch of cave men? You want to go out in the woods and live like Pineys, go ahead. Not me. I like money. Money is what I live for." Then he spit on the floor and rubbed it in good with his shoe. Afterwards, he hopped on his forklift, fired up the propane, and squealed the tires down the dock.

I looked around and saw the other faces looking at me. Evidently, the others agreed with Eddie. "Well, I still think money sucks," I said, trying to brush off the encounter, trying to hold my own in this rhetorical arena. Only Mario gave me a friendly shrug, pulled me aside and said, "Think about it. If you didn't have no money, how could you buy beer?" His agile mind had cut right through my pompous rhetoric. I shuffled through my bills of lading and headed off to find twenty four cases of Mr. Clean.

By the fifth night of work, conversation had turned to women. There wasn't much that I didn't know about sex but somehow the talk on the dock made me feel like I had grown up with all the wrong notions. Somehow, along the trials and tributaries of my adolescent love-life, I had acquired the foolish notion in my head that love and sex were somehow mixed up together.

Bill Fadimen was the trailer jockey. He was the guy who shuttled trailers around outside from door to door. When one was filled, he'd hook up a tractor, pull it away and bring in another to be loaded. It was a position that commanded respect from a mere dock worker. Bill had probably lectured often before on the subject but he caught up with me on the issue of women at lunch on the fifth day. And while others around me dozed or ate Cheese Whiz sandwiches or, miraculously did both at the same time, Bill sat down beside me and began to get a few things off his chest.

"I got a wife and two kids," he said. "And this shit job. If Reno Allen don't die, I'm gonna be stuck on the night shift for my life." Reno was the daytime counterpart for Billy. "Don't never get married."

"I don't believe in marriage," I answered. Finally I had someone more or less on my level, I figured. I wanted to say that if two people loved each other, they didn't need anything legal or formal. I wasn't into legal and formal stuff. But I did believe in love.

"You're a smart kid," Billy said. He slugged back something from a thermos that I think was orange juice and vodka. "You know why I got married?"

"Why?"

"Because I was a dumb shit. And she had tits out to here." Billy showed me with his hands where *here* was.

"Now I got two screaming brats and an old lady who does nothing but watch TV and spend my jesus money."

I wanted to ask him if he knew anything about birth

control. Or maybe I was going to try my anti-money rap on him, tell him to quit his job and move to Alaska and homestead. He had been out jockeying trailers before when I had given my little attempt at wholesale societal revolution before. But I kept my mouth shut.

"Do you believe I actually thought I was in love with the bitch? What a crock. There's no such thing as love," Billy pointed out. "Fuck 'em and forget 'em."

I had heard the anthem before.

"I knew that, too, knew it better than anyone," Billy continued, "but then one day something came over me. I don't know what it was. I swear I don't. It was like somebody shoved me into it. It was part her, but it was me, too. Yeah, and I even knew better. I'd seen my old man, I'd seen Eddie and all those other dumb fucks get married. But I fucking knew better."

"Maybe you did the right thing. Maybe it's just a bad phase right now."

Billy slugged back the O.J. I could tell from the wet brightness in his eyes that it was certainly laced with something. "My life is one long bad phase, kid. I'm telling you this for your own good. You go out and get a piece of ass and get it good. You're just a skinny little kid, but you can probably find something to get into. Women'll fall for all sorts of crap. I've seen 'em go for skinny guys."

What was I supposed to think, that he was giving me good advice or that this was some sort of backhanded compliment? All the other guys in the lunch room were conked out asleep. Bill and I were the only ones awake. I wanted to end the discussion. I thought plenty about love and sex and for me, the two were intrinsically tied together. Deep down, I was a romantic. Lust and love went together for me, inseparably. Billy was bad news in a fifty point typeface. He was staring at me, waiting for me to say something like, "Yeah, man. Sex is all that matters. No such thing as love." But even in my late-night-early morning near-comatose state, I was feeling riled at this asshole. I had heard Billy outjive everyone on the loading platform about fuck-ups. He could talk about how many fuck-ups he knew for hours if given a chance. And now, something was becoming clear. He was the expert. He was the world's greatest fuck-up who had first hand knowledge from the inside.

But I was going to let it slide, not open my mouth. I tried closing my eyes to pretend that I would power nap with the little time left from a disconsolate lunch. But Bill couldn't let it rest. He had read my mind.

"You wanna know what love is? Love is bullshit."

I opened my eyes and stared into the bleary eyes of the demon, the antichrist. I no longer felt sorry for Bill. I was too angry.

At moments like this I have a bad habit of speaking absurd little profundities that don't suit the discussion. I looked him square in the face and said it: "Love, you shit head, is not bullshit." I had been in love with maybe a dozen young women. They all had, in one way or another, trampled me, broken my heart, left me bleeding in the gutters. But I still believed in love, no matter how much it had fucked me over. I wanted to explain all that but I didn't have the chance.

I saw Bill's arm swing out away from his body. He threw his thermos on the floor. I didn't flinch. I assumed he was going to plant a big one in my face. I didn't care. But he crooked his arm and locked his elbow around my neck until I was bent over into a headlock.

"You little shit. What the hell do you know about it?"

I gathered deep inner strength and the profounder peace of that comes with inner purpose. I said nothing, made no resistance lest he break my neck. I could feel the power of this truck jockey's arm, sense the immense pent-up rage of someone who felt the world had cheated him out of everything good.

"You're lying. Tell me it's bullshit!" he insisted.

Not a squeak. All the boys were awake now. Mario was

coming to my rescue. Bill locked on harder. "You think you gotta rescue this faggot?" he asked Mario, stopping him in his tracks. Mario backed off. Maybe he was afraid Bill would bust my neck or maybe he couldn't handle the idea of being associated with someone accused of being a faggot. In Bill's spit-fried brain, anyone who didn't ascribe to the fuck 'em and forget 'em code was clearly not a male heterosexual. The logic was obvious, like a urine stain on a white porcelain floor. "Say it!" Bill insisted again, his voice almost crackling with rage.

My mind was racing. Here I was about to die in defense of love in the abstract, the very concept of romantic love between a man and a woman, the last bastion of the finest of human creeds. I said nothing. I would not give in.

And then Clarence, the dispatcher, appeared in the doorway. He leaned against the frame and shook his head, saw the maniacal look in Billy Fadiman's eyes. Then he looked at me, my face turning shades of the rainbow from lack of oxygen. "Say it," Clarence said in a non-commital voice.

I tried to look around me but my head was locked too tight. "Sure, Billy," I said. "It's bullshit." But I spoke the words in such a way that Billy and everybody else knew what I meant. I hadn't given in but I'd given Bill a way out. He didn't want to lose his job over this. He let go. Lunch was over.

"Get back to work," Clarence said, shaking his head.

Soon after that I was laid off for two weeks. Business was slow at North Penn Transfer. Mario, No Doz, and I were the most recently hired so we were given the temporary boot. When the fall traffic of goods started up again in August, we were called back and it was even harder re-adjusting to the night shift again.

There was a good chance that the company was about to be bought out by a larger trucking outfit and everyone on the dock was nervous. Many would lose their jobs if not their seniority. For guys like Billy, even if he didn't get canned, it might mean he'd never get a daylight shift in his life. Things were tense on the loading platforms. There was always too much work now for the small, beleaguered army that we were and we worked harder, in hopes, I suppose, that the company would not be sold, that the present owners would see enough profit in it to stick it out.

And then one hot, armpit-dripping night in late August we were all working at top speed. The lights had attracted mosquitoes inside. There were dozens of oversize barrels of pesticide to be loaded. Cartons were piled ceiling high and it was imperative that we had everything ready to go by eight o'clock the next morning. The dayshift guys were getting pissed-off at us for not getting done on time. Dayshift guys had it easy, we all knew, and they could dump on us any time they wanted.

Billy was out in the yard jockeying, shifting hard, jamming gears, pulling trailers in and out of slots at a frightening pace. Inside, Eddie was working with No Doz on a forty-footer that Bill had just backed in, uncoupled from the truck and moved on. I saw No Doz wheel the first carton of airplane parts into the front end of the trailer. He rolled up the ramp and on down the tunnel of the forty-foot trailer. Hot on his heels was Eddie on the forklift with a skid of black roofing tar in twenty gallon cans.

I think all of us on the dock saw what happened next out of the corner of our eyes. Eddie was speeding up the metal ramp, the claws of the lift were just reaching into the back of the trailer. Then the trailer began to move. In slow motion it rolled away from the edge of the loading ramp, pushed on by the momentum of Eddie's speeding forklift. The trailer rolled out into the yard, out into the darkness. The forklift tipped forward and Eddie screamed.

We all ran to the loading bay. A machine, maybe two tons in weight, had just fallen four feet onto the ground with a man aboard. Mario was the first to the door and he jumped off. There was the forklift lying sideways in the gravel. Eddie was lying in the dirt. His face was tightened up into a knot. He let out another long wail and walked out into the darkness. I can't say for sure, but I think he was crying. But he was alive.

Clarence was running over to the door now. He saw Eddie on the ground, the forklift on it's side. "Holy shit! Where's No Doz?"

The truck had rolled out into the yard. Someone grabbed the emergency flashlight from the wall and shined it out towards the open trailer. There was No Doz, flat up against the front wall of the trailer, his arms out in a crucifix position and scared-shitless written all over his face.

"You okay?" Clarence yelled.

No Doz nodded.

Mario was now helping Eddie up onto he platform. Eddie was finishing up with being scared to death and translating it into violent rage. "I could have been killed," he shouted to Clarence. "What happened?" Clarence demanded, looking around at all of us. No one said a word. Insects smashed against the lights overhead in an awful racket.

Eddie was breathing hard. No Doz was still glued to the wall of the trailer, eyes wide-open for once.

"I'll tell you what fucking happened," Eddie sputtered. "Jerk Face out there in the yard forgot to set the brake. I'll break his fucking face."

Just then Billy came walking up the metal steps from outside. He knew something had happened but he didn't know exactly what.

Eddie lunged for him and caught him off guard, throwing him onto a pile of chain metal fencing. Eddie was trying to grab onto Billy's throat, and Billy was trying to save his windpipe from the angry Greek claws.

Clarence and Mario had to pull the two apart. Eddie's glasses flew onto the concrete and broke. Again Eddie seemed on the verge of tears. "I could have been killed," he said again to Clarence. "Because of that jerk."

Billy lunged this time but was held back by Mario. "Take the night off," he said to Eddie. "Go home and get some rest. "Everybody else, take a break." Clarence put his arm around Eddie and led him off toward his car. The others filed into the lunchroom, shaken and nervous as speed freaks.

I was left alone on the dock with Billy who seemed like a pet dog who had just been kicked across the street.

"Wasn't my fault," he said. "Some of those trucks don't have good brakes. I set that brake. That damn Greek didn't have any right to accuse me of fucking up."

I wanted to help Billy up but I knew that he'd be ready to slam into whatever came in the way of the pent-up rage he felt. He had been kicked around again, and according to his law, he would kick around whatever he had a chance to get at. I threw up my hands in the air; I wasn't accusing or comforting. I could see that Billy had to live with himself and that was maybe one of the hardest things any human could endure.

My shirt was sticking to my chest. I had a dozen mosquitoes sucking blood from both arms. It was three o'clock in the morning and I wanted to be home in bed. As I drifted towards the lunch room, I kept thinking about what it must feel like to be Billy from the inside. I had seen it in his yes and it haunted me as I tried to nap. All that hurt and all that hate inside one skull trying to make it in a world where love doesn't exist. I could see that his was the hardest job going for anybody on the night shift. And I knew that when summer was over and I was returned to the flipside of this dark life, I wanted to live among daylight people and, even if all the evidence proved otherwise, I was going to hang onto a belief in love like it was a goddamn religion.

27

Mid-Life Calm

The mystery lies all around. Science would have answers but not always truth. Start with the potholes in the road. They bloom in spring. As do fires on hillsides. Year after year. People with large, mostly unused tracts of land burn off the dead grass from last year. A wind sneaks up on them and soon the flames lick beyond broom-handle control. Someone calls the fire department but soon the burning grass has taken the house and parts of the natural neighbourhood. Too late the trucks come roaring down the road like demented wildebeests. Through it all the potholes are unaffected.

If I had a true sense of what goes on out there, I wouldn't write about it. I understand very little, therefore continue to record, to explain, even if my explanations are temporary, even if I don't fully understand the plot. Miracles are all around. I'm astounded, baffled, amazed. If I had all the answers, boredom would ensue. Then death.

How do you know when you are about to die? When you finally have all the tools you need.

I'm repairing a rocking chair made in Sweden. Suddenly I discover a screw with an unrecognizable head. It requires a new tool, something that probably every householder in Scandinavia owns. Vice grips won't work. Neither will Allen wrenches. (One day in Canadian Tire I bought a complete set of Allen wrenches. I thought my life was complete. I already owned several slot screwdrivers, a quiver of Phillips head screwdrivers, and even a trio of Robertsons, but now I was ready for anything.)

Then came the Scandinavian chair. There are thousands of tools out there yet required for living. Death is far away. Much is to be learned and acquired. Those of us who are not still searching for a home somewhere on this planet are yet trying to make their homes complete.

My last book found little comfort when searching for a home in Halifax. A knowledgeable editor returned it. Said she mistrusted anything that smacked of autobiography.

The implication was simple: books need to be made from a complex set of evasive maneuvers. Above all: never write about your own life. One's own life is diminutive. To write about it is vain and ultimately boring. History is fair territory, as long as one works at arm's length.

Yet I was certain my life had noteworthy moments of glory and woe and humor, my ego notwithstanding.

This morning my daughter wanted confirmation of a fact. "What's the highest age anyone has ever lived?" she asked.

My wife is reading a book about longevity and had produced the fact at breakfast just recently. One hundred and twenty, possibly one hundred and thirty. I told Sunyata the statistic. She was impressed.

"Why does anyone bother dying at just ninety, then?"

Time stretched out like a circus eternity for my eight-year-old. Life would go on just as it is now forever. She knew I worried over nuclear war but was confident I had the ability to put an end to it if the death of civilization was at hand.

That's part of why I stopped writing fiction, for a while at least. It was too easy to fix the world through fiction. I had all the right tools. But somehow the job was never good enough to leak over into real life.

If I found a nuclear weapon right now, for example, if one fell off a cruising bomber and didn't detonate, or if one washed ashore from a Trident submarine, what would I do with it? With the proper skills and knowledge, and, of course, tools, I could dismantle one at least, assert my will over the arms race. How many differently sized Allen wrenches would it require? How many sockets and wrenches? Would I snip the red or the blue wire and what about the highly sophisticated anti-tampering device? Or would I simply be up against that Scandinavian screwhead that defies vice grips and all the tools in Canadian Tire?

I wouldn't turn it over to the government. Instead, I would phone up my friend who owes me several refrigerator-carrying favors. On his behalf, I've heaved and hauled a mid-sized freezer and three refrigerators. Providing there was no radiation leakage, I'd ask Mike to come help me load the nuclear warhead or MIRV footprint bomb into a small dory and I'd paddle it out to sea. I don't know how far I'd go before my arms give out. Since I'd be incapable of throwing it overboard, I'd chop a hole in the boat so it could fall into the deep.

Then I'd have to paddle home. I would have my surfboard along. On calm, sunny days, I'm capable of paddling long distances on my knees, a skill I acquired when I was fourteen years old and living in New Jersey. The Jersey Shore was not a bad place to learn a life-sustaining skills like knee-paddling in those early days of the Vietnam War.

I was never drafted for Vietnam. My number was 183 in the lottery. That put me half-way down the list. A number was attached to every day of the year and you were assigned a number according to your birthday. Mine was March 21 which had logged in at 183. That year they never got past a hundred and forty something. I never really got to the point of sweating it. Luck was with me even then.

This week I learned that they are building missile casings in Lunenburg, Nova Scotia. Lunenburg is one of the most beautiful, quiet little fishing towns in the world. The people making the bomb casings do it because they need the work. We are all savages when it comes to income.

Not long ago I was on a side road not far from Bliss, New Brunswick, driving on to Fredericton through territory guaranteed to produce for me the vision of a straggly, spring moose swimming raging rivers. All around, the St. John River floods usurped land until the highway was a thin isthmus of land.

Along the road a family was stopped. Three kids and a grandparent. Each was carrying a colander. They were picking things up from the ground and putting small items into the colander. The ground was littered with square glass jewels of safety glass, automotive molding, and broken tail lights.

Most of the wreckage had been hauled away but here was a family searching through the aftermath for a wedding ring or a small fragment of a past. I was incapable of stopping to help. I drove on. The flooded woodlands were full of "wonderful and bedraggled moose," as my friend had said. I was to be on the lookout for them. Then I was to stay, all expenses paid, at a motel in Fredericton, along a part of town that looked exactly like New Jersey. The motel would have an indoor swimming pool, a hot tub, a sauna, and an ice machine that worked all night long making ice until it pushed open the icemaker door and spilled it out onto the floor.

Not far beyond the accident site, at a mailbox that carried the name, Cecil Machete, I stopped for gas. A man walked toward the car in overalls, wiping his hand on a rag that was shiny with use.

"Fill it with unleaded," I said.

The man began to curse and spit on the ground. He removed the gas cap gently from my car, but then began to kick the gas pump. He cursed long and loud, turning briefly into some violent inhuman creature. He attacked the pump with a greasy fist.

At long last it hummed into life and the man returned to human form. "You just have to reason with it," he told me, smiling politely.

I gave him a twenty for the gas and followed him inside for the change. Men were sipping Cokes and talking about fish.

"Do you have any road maps?" I asked. I'm a big fan of road maps, even when I know my way.

The attendant yanked a display of maps off the wall, rack, screws and all, from behind him. "Which one you want?"

I looked at the three holes he had left in the old plaster wall, saw that the road maps were $3.95 each.

"I guess I was looking for the free kind," I told him.

The men with Cokes and fishing all laughed and looked at me like I had just told them all that I planned on sleeping with each of their mothers.

I accepted my change and left. Things like this happen when you drive alone through unknown territory. Maps, above all things, should be free. Destinations can be costly, but the way there should be free, marked clearly with colorful lines.

A few miles down the road, I found a wooden covered bridge on a side gravel road. I pulled my car up inside and looked out of a window in the center of the bridge that someone had chainsawed out of the wall. The river was framed by it. Not a moose appeared. A brief albeit heroic sun popped out so that zebra light streaked the inner darkness of the bridge. It was just about then that the loneliness set in. Maybe it was the result of the family with colanders among the safety glass jewels, foraging along the side of the road for something very important lost in an accident where, I was certain, someone had died.

Earlier that morning I had driven through Stewiake, Nova Scotia. A massive billboard on the highway proclaimed Stewiake as being located exactly halfway between the pole and the equator.

At thirty-seven, I too figured I was halfway between something. Not just birth and death but between childhood and old age. Now, several hundred miles beyond Stewiake, and somewhere slightly north of the halfway mark between the pole and the equator, I was alone inside a covered bridge looking out at a small garrulous river. Even now, despite the loneliness building up like a cold stone in my chest, I wanted the middle of my life to stretch out forever. Beginnings, I knew from experience, were tumultuous, unsettling but necessary. Endings were forever unsatisfactory. The only thing that ever counted was the middle, the halfway point to somewhere, the feeling of having come this far and knowing that there is farther yet to go.